BROUGHT TO YOU BY THE FO...
UNCHAIN YOUR INNER ST...
MARIA C. KRAUSE

Unchain

AUTHENTIC
SOUL

HOW 12 REAL WOMEN
TURNED THEIR DEEPEST
PAIN AND FEARS
INTO SUPERPOWERS

A COLLECTION OF 12 UNIQUE LIFE STORIES INSPIRING YOU TO FALL IN LOVE
WITH YOUR AUTHENTIC SELF AND START LIVING LIFE ON YOUR TERMS.

Unchain Your AUTHENTIC

SOUL

A COLLECTION OF 12 UNIQUE LIFE STORIES INSPIRING YOU TO FALL IN LOVE WITH YOUR AUTHENTIC SELF AND START LIVING LIFE IN YOUR TERMS.

FOREWORD

Perception,

The ability to see, hear or become aware of something through the senses.

Pain is life's most valuable teacher. It reminds us that we are humans, and as humans, we feel. Through pain, we discover that we are indeed, worthy of so much more in life than constant suffering. We discover that we are entitled to be happy, to feel joy, and to do something that brings meaning and purpose to our lives.

Every day of your life is a new day to start over. You get a new chance to reinvent yourself and start truly living.

Each and every one of us have gone through our own share of disappointments, pain, and challenges but these are not reasons to give up; on the contrary, we are capable of turning our life events into our biggest strengths.

FOREWORD

Looking at things from a different perspective can immensely help us understand that everything we go through has a purpose and meaning, no matter how awful and painful might be at the time, there is always light after darkness. Sunshine after a storm. Laughs after tears. Hope after despair. Life after self-destruction. Love after loathing.

Every day is a new day to become the woman you were born to be… Every day is your chance to live a free and joyful life, on your own terms.

Unchain Your Authentic Soul Lovey, the world needs your greatness.

Your Soul Sister,

Maria C. Krause. XXX

SYNOPSIS

"WHAT ONE FEARS CAN STRENGTHEN, CAN HEAL"

— CLARISSA PINKOLA ESTES, PH. D., AND
AUTHOR OF WOMEN WHO RUN WITH THE
WOLVES

Unchain Your Authentic Soul is a collection of 12 unique and powerful life stories from real women who have experienced everything that life has to offer. Pain. Fear. Doubts. Success. Happiness. Love. Joy. Heartbreak. Self-destruction. Re-birth. Self-acceptance….and infinite self-love.

These are real women, just like you, who through their deepest pain and fears they got to discover their Authentic Soul.

These amazing women are opening their hearts to you. They are here to remind you that you are not alone… There is someone in this world who understands you and accepts you for the beautiful, amazing woman that you are.

SYNOPSIS

Life is beautiful, and you have it in you to choose how magical you want yours to be.

Set your Soul Free!

Let it rise!

Let it shine!

CONTENTS

SUPERHERO YOU

BY ANDREAH BARKER

"A hero is somebody who voluntarily walks into the unknown."

— TOM HANKS

Be the Hero of Your Own Story

For the longest time, I think I was subconsciously looking for someone to save me. Someone bigger and stronger and smarter and more attractive and more successful to come along and say, "Hey, you can stop worrying now. I got your back!"

Actually, this person didn't have to be a person at all. It could be a partner, but it could also come in the form of a job or a book deal, or the winning lottery ticket. It didn't matter really. It was that one thing or that one person, who would recognize all of the good that I was trying to do in the world and reward me for it.

Don't get me wrong here, it wasn't that I didn't want to work hard or create something that was authentically mine or leave this world far better off than it was before. No, that wasn't it at all. I had, and still do have passions and dreams that drive me every single moment of every single day. The difference now is that I've recog-nized my subconscious desire to be saved and I know where it came from. It came from my inability to believe in my own ability to succeed at anything. Seriously anything!

I didn't believe in myself and so I thought I needed to be saved. Well, to be honest that particular insight didn't come to me until recently. I didn't put two and two together until I started thinking about what I wanted to share in this book. What story did I have of great triumph? I wavered between this and that and this and that, but for the most part, I have considered my life to be pretty average. I've experienced loss, grief, disappointments, and failures, but I've also lived a life filled with love, joy, opportunity, passion, and adventure. So, how would the story I share even come close to some of those you will or have most certainly read in this book?

I didn't know. I started one outline and I scraped it. I started another and went so far as to write a page and then left it stewing for a week. It wasn't right. Why was I so stuck on what to write for this book? When you feel stuck in your writing, or have what you think might be writer's block, I would actually argue that you are not stuck at all. You are in the process. You are thinking through your options and haven't landed on the one yet. The one that hits you in the heart and says: "Heyyyyy, this is it, girl! You HAVE to write about this." You know it right away. This is the moment you've been waiting for.

Sometimes that moment feels like that, but sometimes it feels more like a soft river flowing over you, that softly pulls you along with it until you're ready to begin. That is more like what happened for me here.

Have you ever caught yourself thinking:

If I could just get that one audition, it would catapult my career on Broadway.
If I could get that one job, I wouldn't have to worry about my bills ever again.
If only a publisher would see the brilliance in my writing and offer me the deal of a lifetime.
If I got that one huge promotion my career would be on the fast track.
If I could meet the love of my life, I would have a teammate to walk by my side.

I have to admit, I have thought things like this often in my life, but I never really processed in my brain that I was actually looking to be saved. I didn't make the direct connection. When I realized it, it hit me like a ton of bricks. "That's such bullshit," I thought to myself. "I don't need to be saved. Only victims need to be saved, and I am no victim!"

This got me thinking about when in my life I actually shifted my thinking. From needing to be saved to taking control of my life. As I did, I realized that I am a superhero. I am the superhero of my own life, and that one defining moment, although it's not the only defining moment, sent me on a path to living a life filled with love, curiosity, wonder, joy, and magic.

My Superhero Origin Story

Every superhero has an origin story. Whether you like Marvel or DC or your favorite superhero lives in this world, they have a story. You have a story. I have a story.

This is the story of how I discovered my superpowers:

There once was a girl in this world. She wasn't as young as she used to be. She wondered and she wished, and she dreamed. She wasn't happy to do what she was told. She wasn't happy to just get through the day.

"There has to be more," she thought to herself one day as she sat in the park on her way to work.

As she sat, she thought more and as she thought more, she wondered. She wondered if she was holding herself back. She wondered why she was taught to pick a career and then never, ever, ever change her mind. She felt stuck, she felt tired. And she never quit. But as the tears began to flow, she knew something wasn't right.

For the past couple of years, she had been taking her writing more seriously. She still viewed it as a hobby, something that she absolutely loved doing, but thought she could never make money at. She, for now, let's call her Sadie, had been submitting short stories to a contest in the Toronto Star in the hope of winning. If she won, her writing would be validated. If she won that top prize it would save her.

Somewhere deep-down Sadie knew this way of thinking was actually stopping her. It took some time for her to really understand what she wanted and that what she wanted was in fact possible.

What Sadie was lacking the most was an unwavering belief in herself and her ability to make her dreams a reality. But she didn't know this yet. She didn't know she had everything within her to achieve what she wanted to in this life. A big part of Sadie's problem was that deep down she believed she wasn't destined for big things. That was for other people: the brilliant people, the wealthy people, the famous people.

So, she continued on until one day she couldn't anymore.

Her career hadn't given her the stability she thought it would by this time. Sadie had convinced herself that what she needed was to have more stability in her life, and she took an office job in the film industry. There was so much creativity happening around her, but it wasn't hers to create. She thought that being surrounded by creativity would be enough. She couldn't have been more wrong.

In the midst of it all, tragedy struck, and her world changed. Each day it became harder to get up. On the days when she wasn't blind-sided by overwhelming sadness, she walked through each moment as if surrounded by a heavy thick fog. Everything was grey. And although she knew she had so much to be grateful for in her life, she struggled to find the joy in anything.

So, Sadie wrote. It was the one thing that helped pull her brain out of the downward spiral or as she called it: the loop of bullshit. The loop of bullshit is an angry thought pattern that takes hold of her being and makes the world around her vibrate with hatred. It would overwhelm her completely. It felt as though the universe was against her and there was nothing, she could do in this world to make anything better.

Sadie knew her options were simple: continue to get up every day or not. There was something deep within that wanted her to continue to get up. Not only that, but she also wanted to do so much more. She wanted to be excited about life again. She wanted to feel that passion she once had for what she was doing.

And so, Sadie wrote. She wrote every morning on the train to work. She wrote about a girl named Sadie who didn't know what she wanted to do with her life. This was her. She had once known what she wanted to do with all the days of all of her life, and one day, she didn't anymore.

In Sadie's story, she confronted her fear in order to see the beauty in the world again. She met the good wolf, who was young and wise beyond his years. He helped her to see where she needed to go.

Here is a part of the journey she wrote after meeting the Good Wolf:

Sadie looked up. The steps near the top looked treacherous. She wasn't scared. There was no turning back now. She wondered if Wolf was still down there, watching her continue on her quest. She thought back as she navigated her way up, and marvelled at his wisdom. How could someone so young know so much?

Wolf had helped her realize with each step she is already being.

She is being the girl who met the moon and learned that it was possible to have more than one dream. She is being the girl who experienced the magic of the ocean by simply letting go and trusting herself. She is being the girl who spent each moment of each day doing her best to feed the good, wise, empathetic, joyful, hopeful wolf so that the mean, angry, ignorant wolf wouldn't ever win. She is the girl who knows exactly what she'll wish for when she meets the stars next. She is the girl who is excited to tell her story so that one day others will take the chance and climb the cliff stairs too.

Once Sadie reached the end of her story, a new day unfolded. She knew exactly what she wanted to do; Sadie wanted to write, and she believed it was possible. She believed it was possible because in her writing journey she learned that the stars she wished on, the moon she marvelled at, the dancing colours of the ocean, and the sun that shone through her window as it awoke, were all rooting for her.

They were all there saying: "Hey, I'm here to help you fight the fog. I'm here when you need more strength to turn the anger and the hatred into light and love."

It was in this journey of self-discovery that Sadie uncovered her superpower. The big one. The superpower that makes the world an even better place than it already is. Is it writing? Storytelling? Creativity? Yes, to all of them. Those are all skills she possesses, but they only contribute to her superpower. Her big superpower is letting the light through the fog. It is in her stories of magic and adventure. It is in her ability to help others see the strength in the stories they share. She uses her power for good.

When Sadie finished writing her book, Sadie: A Story About A Girl Who Just Didn't Know, she knew exactly what actions she needed to take. This is when her writing company, Sadie Tells Stories was born.

* * *

The Journey Continues

The thing about life is that it's not all about happily ever after. At the end of a movie where the girl gets the guy and the credits begin to roll as the camera pans over their embrace to a beautiful sunset beyond, I always imagine this scene followed by a lifetime of bliss. There are no more trials. There are no more struggles. It's just endless joy. Every single moment of every single day is complete happiness. They have arrived.

We all know this isn't true. There will always be ups and downs. There will always be wrought to do. This isn't a bad thing. It's all about perspective. Since starting Sadie Tells Stories, I've shifted the focus of my work many times. From being a writer who took a variety of work, to being a ghostwriter and coach who helps her clients realize their book dreams, to understanding who my ideal client is, to setting clear boundaries; I have used each new lesson to define what I am creating. What I am creating is ever-evolving because I am ever-evolving.

Right in this very moment as I type these words, I am creating a life that is filled with creativity, joy, love, and freedom. Over the past year, I embarked on a journey to understand how I was stopping myself from creating this life. I began by looking at the areas of my life where when asked how I felt about them, my response was that it was *fine*.

What?!? There is no part of me that wants my gravestone to read: "It was fine." So why then at the beginning of each day was I choosing *fine*? What exactly does *fine* mean?

When I quickly looked up the definition of *fine*, I was a bit surprised! It actually means that something is of a fine quality. Something is of a satisfactory or pleasing manner. Okay, okay… but… I know for me when I say something is *fine*… I mean that it'll do. I know that I'm saying I'll settle for it. It's not the best, but it'll work.

I feel like most people don't mean that they are really happy when they say, "it's fine." This is what the urban dictionary had to say:

What someone says when they're feeling like shit. They don't want to tell why they feel like shit and feel like hiding.

"How are you doing? You look sad today."

"I'm doing fine. Thanks..."

Yep, that sounds about right! So, when you're saying your life is *fine* what you're actually saying is that your life feels like shit, but you don't want to admit it or deal with it. You have chosen to settle.

As I worked at growing a business that made my soul sing and my heart fill with love, more and more I needed to remove the Settle Moments.

You know the ones. In business or in your career it's when you choose the safe route: the job that will pay the bills, or the demanding client because you don't know where the next one is going to come from. In love, it's when you end up settling for a partner who doesn't understand what you need, but you stay because it's better than being alone. In life, it's choosing laundry over a day in the park or saving money over the opportunity for an epic adventure. Yes, some days you have to do laundry, but some-times you have to let go of what you should do and do what you want to do!

Anything worth doing has never been described as *fine* or *okay*, and yet we regularly go about our average lives choosing to settle for careers, relationships, and experiences that are both of those things.

Don't get me wrong, I'm not saying that every single moment of every single day is meant to be epic, fantastic, mind-blowing, orgasmic (although, let's be honest, more of that wouldn't hurt), inspiring, passionate, or filled with so much happiness you'll burst. If all of life was on high speed and required full energy, you'd burn out in a heartbeat.

No, some moments need to be quiet, rejuvenating, boring, disap-pointing, unexpected, and even heartbreaking. These aren't the moments I'm talking about. These moments are necessary fuel for the epic, fantastic, mind-blowing, orgasmic, inspiring, passionate or filled with so much happiness you'll burst moments. The moments I'm talking about are the ones when you settle. You make a choice for something less than what your authentic self truly desires.

SETTLE moments are the ones when you actively make a choice to not go for the big dream.

SETTLE moments happen when you allow yourself to be persuaded by your doubts.

SETTLE moments happen when you allow yourself to be controlled by your fears.

SETTLE moments happen when you allow yourself to be abused by your low confidence levels.

SETTLE moments happen when you allow yourself to be guided solely by the needs of others.

SETTLE moments stop you from going for the promotion.

SETTLE moments stop you from starting your own business.

SETTLE moments stop you from asking your crush out on a date.

SETTLE moments stop you from getting out of an abusive relationship.

SETTLE moments stop you from experiencing life.

SETTLE moments strengthen all things that are *okay* and *fine* about your life.

SETTLE moments bring about the death of all living dreams.

Yep, anything magical, wonder-filled, and joy-inducing is so, so much more than *fine* will ever be. Seriously… so much MORE!

* * *

A Year of Curiosity, Magic and Saying Yes

The whole idea for LIVING began originally as a book outline. Truthfully, I was 2 chapters into a completely different book and it just wasn't flowing. As I sat at my computer mindlessly reading the last paragraph I had written, a new idea popped into my head. My gut response was to stop it. I needed to focus. But something kept pulling me towards this new idea. So, I quickly opened a new note and typed as fast as my brain worked. Within 10 minutes I had the full rough skeleton for a 10-chapter book called LIVING.

I was filled with excitement. The kind of excitement only a new idea brings. I knew I had to write this book and I had to do it right then and there, and so it was with a bit of sadness that I put my other book aside.

"Go with the flow," I reminded myself.

I have never been happier that I did.

LIVING became so much more than just a book; it became a way of building on the life I had been creating in a new and meaningful way. As I wrote I explored the world around me, at a time when the most I could really do was take my new puppy to the park, because the world was in hiding.

As the world around me changed, I focused on the magic of all that surrounded me. I got curious about how I could create magic, not only for myself but for my readers too. This curiosity led me to saying *yes* to what I truly love and making it a priority. Once I said *yes*, the work I needed to do on myself, shifted.

I decided that in order to continue to establish an unwavering belief in myself, my life, and the world around me, I needed to do the following:

Live in the now.

Live in love.

Live in abundance.

Live in curiosity.

Live in wonder.

Live in YES!

Doing all of these things helped me to see the magic in myself, my life, and the world around me. Most importantly it helped me to find and own my superpower. For the rest of this chapter, I want to share with you a few things I learned in my exploration of LIVING.

* * *

Live in YES

This is a big one! I had no idea how much I was saying *no* to things before I even gave them a real chance. Or, on the flip side, how much I was saying *yes* to things that didn't serve me in order to please others.

Living in YES, doesn't mean saying *yes* all of the time. It means saying *no* sometimes to make room in your life for the *yes* that's right for you. It all comes down to the idea of not choosing some-thing that will stop you from living a life that makes your soul sing with joy and your body dance all of the happy dances all over your house.

One of the big things I said *yes* to this summer was a 3-week vaca-tion. When I was preparing to leave I had gathered all of the info I needed to work forward on two books for clients, but as soon as we arrived I knew I needed to stop, take a breath, enjoy nature and simply just be with my family. I took a break and didn't work. It was the longest vacation of my adult life.

Do you know what happened? ...Nothing. My clients understood. No one was angry. I came back ready and happy to be home. I said *yes* to me, and now I am in an even better place for myself, my family, and my clients.

One of the big things I've said *no* to is taking on clients just to pay the bills. Many times, over the past 3 years in the business I have said *yes* to work out of fear; fear that I wouldn't be able to get anything else and would have to close up shop. The most valuable lesson I've learned in taking small work that didn't pay well is that it stopped me from growing. It achieved the exact opposite of what I intended, and many times almost forced me to quit because there was no time in the day left to grow.

I ask you this:

1. What are you saying *yes* to out of fear or a desire to please others?

2. What are you saying *no* to that you would love to say *yes* to?

Live in Curiosity

For me, curiosity goes beyond my desire to learn Spanish or to understand how blockchain technology works or to draw a bird really well. It's about taking it a step further. For example, with blockchain technology, I am curious about how it can be used to make wealth accessible for everyone. Or with understanding how to draw a bird really well it's so that I can create my own kind of bird to live in one of my stories.

Curiosity, for me, is about ideas. All ideas. Big ones. Small ones. Random ones. Ideas that fly at you from left field. Any idea. I love brainstorming. The ones that get me excited are the ones that break my brain. These are the moments I am truly curious about explor-ing. You know them. You've felt them. It feels like you are on the verge of a breakthrough, but you don't know exactly how-to break-through. Yet, you keep going even though you don't know exactly where you're headed.

My version of exploring curiosity is in developing a new magical world for another book I'm writing. This is what I've also said *yes* to making more time for in my life. It's the unwavering belief in myself that has allowed me to do it. Because I believe that the world needs a whole lot more of my version of magic, just like it needs a whole lot more of your version of magic too.

I ask you this:

1. What is one thing you are curious about that you've stopped yourself from exploring?

2. If you said *yes* to exploring that thing, how would it allow you to share even more magic with the world?

* * *

Live in Love

Living in love means so much more than the love you share with others. Of course, that kind of love makes the world a better place, but the love I want to talk about in this moment is the love you have for yourself.

For the longest time, decades even, I hated myself. Sometimes this hatred hid within my subconscious and sometimes it was so strong it bubbled to the surface. There were times when I couldn't make eye contact with myself in the mirror. Hating yourself is a horrible feeling.

Living in love has asked me to embrace myself in a way that I never have before. It asks me to love myself with all that have. It asks me to recognize when I can't do it and why. It asks me to learn. It asks me to grow. It asks me to get quiet, even when it's easier to be loud. It asks me to give myself credit for all that I've done, all that I want to do, and all that I am.

Today I love myself more than I ever have before and yet, the work is ongoing. Some days take more self-reflection than others, but I'm happy to report, I don't hate the person looking back at me in the mirror anymore.

I ask you this:

1. Do you truly love yourself?

2. How do you prove to yourself that, that love is authentic?

Your Superhero Origin Story

Living in love, curiosity, and magic in my life began in that one moment when I sat crying on a park bench, even though I didn't know it at the time. I was on the brink of breaking my brain in a way I had never tried to before. Now I am the superhero I always, deep down, knew I could be.

Don't get me wrong. There is wrought to do. Every Superhero has flaws. It's not about arriving. It's not about a happy ending.

It's about being. It's about saying *yes*. It's about loving yourself with all that you have inside you. It's about believing in your own magic. It's about living every single day as your most authentic superhero self!

I ask you this:

1. What is your superhero origin story?

If you haven't written it yet and need some help, here are a few questions to get you started:

1. What was one moment you can remember that changed your life?

2. How did your perspective shift after that moment?

3. Did you know right away, or did it take time?

4. What actions did you take based on?

If you would like to ask me anything about LIVING or want to share your origin story, I would love to hear from you. You can reach me at sadietellsstories@gmail.com.

ABOUT ANDREAH

Andreah Barker is an author, ghost-writer, book coach and solo, kitchen dancer. In the past year, she completed 10 books, 8 full-lengths, and 2 children's books. Her work includes both real-life stories that are intended to motivate real change in the reader's life and fictional tales that aim to inspire the imagination. She loves all things creativity and magic. Working with others to get their stories out into the world is her superpower.

To find out more about her work visit: sadietellsstories.ca

FREEFALLING INTO MY LIFE
BY CEZA OUZOUNIAN

I remember sitting in the library at school trying to decide what to do at university. My school life had pushed me towards a science subject. I was great at maths and science, but my heart wasn't really in it. As I sat there, trying to decide between the 2 options I had narrowed down to, engineering and acting, I thought about which one I *'should'* do.

Engineering? - Easy to get a job in. Stable income. In line with science and maths.

Or Acting? - the unstable one. The job is destined to have a lot of rejection. May not pay enough to live on. Would require a second job to sustain it. However, the rewards would be great - *if I make it.*

What should I do? What is the best option? What do my parents want me to do? Am I good enough to cut it in acting?

Even though my heart wanted to go down the acting pathway, I chose to become an engineer.

University was great. I enjoyed some of the work, I made great friends. I took an interest in aeronautics and decided I would start my career in aerospace and defense.

Or so I thought...

Unlike most people, I hadn't secured a job before leaving university. This bothered me a little, but not enough to stop me from traveling to France and Australia first. I would continue my search for that job after.

After all, I was told by so many different people that it wouldn't be that hard. *"You're a woman, there is positive discrimination in your favor, as they need more women in engineering. You'll get a job no problem."* I actually believed them.

Between 2007 and 2011 I applied for hundreds and hundreds of jobs. I went to many interviews and assessment centers (engineering companies love day long assessments). I was unable to land even a graduate position. I got lots of rejections, each time for a different reason.

I saw friends who were less qualified than me, get work and be successful. I saw people from my year at university get jobs, I knew I was more apt than they were. Why was it so impossible for me to get a job as an engineer? It left me feeling bitter and frus-trated. I didn't want to see friends because I didn't want to explain I still didn't have an engineering job or hear how great they were doing.

In the meantime, I worked at the NHS, the National Health Service in the UK, as an administrator. I worked hard and got promoted to Office Manager, which isn't a bad job, but to be honest, I didn't like it or enjoy it. It was boring, repetitive, and definitely not what I wanted to do. I did have brilliant colleagues and enjoyed working with them, but I didn't want to be there at all. I dreaded going in every day. I used to wish I'd get swine flu, so I didn't have to go to work.

...I didn't get swine flu.

When I wasn't at work, I spent all my time looking for jobs and re-writing my CV or cover letter. Applying for jobs. Becoming increasingly frustrated with the outcomes. Going to interviews. Getting rejected. Searching for jobs. Writing cover letters. Applying for jobs. Feeling desperate. Searching for jobs. Thinking about how to write my cover letter. Applying for jobs. Wondering why I wasn't getting replies. Seeking out how to get the job I wanted. Applying for jobs. Waiting. Going to interviews. Getting rejected.

What else could I do?! It was just a downward spiral; searching, applying, getting rejected, getting more frustrated and upset, over and over. I was trapped in this hellhole.

This was my life. Working in the NHS. Looking for an engineering job. Getting frustrated, annoyed while watching others succeed where I couldn't. The weight on my shoulders feeling heavier and heavier. Questioning if I was good enough at all.

I didn't really want to go out with friends. I wasn't in the mood to go out and socialize. I hated being asked about my job situation. I hated when people kept saying *"Oh, don't worry. There is a job around the corner. The next one will be it."*

I always deflected how I was and my job situations by answering with fake positivity and quickly changing the subject to talk about them. I felt bitter that my friends were progressing in their careers and I wasn't.

I had worries at home also. My gran wasn't in such a good place, it was an easy excuse to say I couldn't go out as I was looking after her. I had the excuse there ready for when I needed it.

I've always been positive, optimistic, and determined, so I powered through not really realizing what was happening. I would find out soon enough.

At the end of 2010, the opportunity came to do an internship in Madrid. I love Spain, I wanted to practice my Spanish and I could get the experience I needed to get an engineering job. This was amazing. It gave me renewed confidence and hope. I remember thinking *"This is it. I'll finally work as an engineer."* I would bounce into work at the NHS with a lightness in my step, I felt care-free and renewed. I would soon be out of the NHS and on my way to a career doing what I had prepared myself through all those years in university.

In February 2011, I packed my bags, said goodbye to my parents, and left for Madrid. I found a flat and moved in. I was to be working at the university in the aerospace department.

Finally, things were looking up.

I went to the university on my first day and met the person who would be my supervisor, he showed me around and got me started. I was excited to be there. They were all really friendly and it was a relaxed environment. I quickly made a few friends.

However, as the weeks went by, I realized that the internship wasn't technical and was geared more towards translation work, which was great work to do. Be as it may, it wasn't giving me the experience I needed. I didn't let that stop me, it was still experience, right? Meanwhile, I kept applying for jobs in Spain and the UK with some of the big companies I wanted to work for.

Then things went downhill. Or rather, this was the beginning of the end of one era, and the start of another.

My birthday is in June. I couldn't afford to go back to London, so my parents said they would pay for my ticket. This made me so happy. I went home on a Friday evening. Saturday was my birthday; I spent an amazing day with my friend. He bought me some shoes for my birthday. Like most women, I LOVE shoes. At one point, I had 60 pairs! I downsized to only 40. I was having a brilliant day. At nightime, I would go home and celebrate with my parents and the following day, with friends. I felt more relaxed and happier than I had for a long time.

That evening, I got home, my dad opened the door and he looked upset and said he had bad news. I walked into the living room and my mum was crying. I realized something terrible had happened. My gran had died that afternoon. She was in Lebanon at the time. By Lebanese tradition the body would have to be buried the next day. My parents were finding it hard to get flights to arrive in Lebanon on time.

Straight away, I went to the computer and found a flight that would get them there in the morning. It was leaving in an hour. They packed as fast as they could, and I drove them to Heathrow Airport. On my drive back, the shock of hearing the news had worn off and I cried the whole way home. I had to be the one to break the news to my younger sister.

I went through different emotions. I was upset as she was the closest person to me to have died. I was upset. I didn't get the chance to see her for one last time. I was also annoyed she had died on my birthday, *"Why couldn't she have waited one more day?"*, I thought while I was crying. I felt guilty for not spending enough time with her, or for the times I hadn't listened when she wanted to tell me some story, or when I didn't do a simple job she had asked me to.

My emotions were in turmoil. I was angry. I was sad. I cried a lot. I downplayed how upset I felt, especially when talking to one of my friends who had lost her mother. I felt that my loss was somewhat lesser than hers, so what I was going through couldn't be as bad. Silly, but that's how I felt at the time.

My brother and a couple of friends came around for my birthday the next day. It felt nice to have familiar company. I made the best lamb kebabs I have ever tasted, but I have no idea how, I wasn't really focusing. I was thinking about my gran.

A few days later I went back to Spain. I must have looked terrible as my supervisor told me to take a few days off.

From then I buckled down and got on with searching and applying for jobs again, as my internship was ending in August.

I moved to a flat that was tiny but much cheaper. It was so tiny; my bedroom was smaller than my current king size bed. I had 3 flat-mates, who were really nice. Juan was one of them who had moved in at the same time as me. We would chat and hang out. And I still had my friends from the university. More than often, I would wear the mask of being happy, when inside I felt the complete opposite, I was sad. But I wasn't going to let a few unfortunate events stop me from trying to be happy. I carried on.

Inside I often felt deflated, sad, tired, and I didn't really want to do anything... but on the outside, I appeared happy and social.

For a short time, things seem to be getting better. I got a few job interviews, including one at Ford.

On the morning of my assessment center with Ford I started feeling incredibly sick. I could barely eat my breakfast. While I was getting dressed, I kept having to stop and sit as I felt like I was going to puke, or worse, come out from the other end. I kept thinking *"Why today? Out of all the days, why am I feeling like this today!?"*

I managed to get dressed. I took a few deep breaths. I felt fragile and nauseous. I kept breathing deep breaths to help me keep the sickness at bay. I gathered my things and made it to the venue.

I had to take a few deep breaths before going in. The whole morning had made me feel unprepared, flushed. I just wanted to curl up in bed. My mind didn't feel clear or focused. I just wanted this day to be over.

Much later I realized this sickness wasn't a coincidence. I was so nervous and desperate to get this job that my gastrointestinal tract was massively affected. All my hopes were pinned on getting this job.

Apart from getting the timings wrong in a group exercise, the rest of the day went fine. I thought I did well. Yes, I wasn't on form, but I did all the tasks well, my interview seemed to have gone well. They always reassure you at these things that they would hire everyone, and this is just a prelim thing. It's not always the case so don't always believe it.

At the end of the assessment center they told us they would decide that evening who had got a job and would contact us later that week or the following, as the job started the month after.

Waiting to hear back was torture. I knew that if I got the job, I would have to know sooner rather than later as it meant moving back to London. When a week and a half had passed, my hopes of getting this job were vanishing, but I was determined to stay posi-tive. I was getting this job, and this was it!

Every day I kept telling myself I had the job. But deep down my gut was saying otherwise. I pushed that feeling down, far down, I wasn't going to listen to it. Not getting this job wasn't an option. I HAD to get it.

I called them to try and find out what was happening. Still nothing.

Three weeks after the assessment centre I got an email to say I didn't get it and that I could arrange a call to get feedback. I still kept my hopes up, and in the meantime, I had applied for a Masters and a job with EADS (European Aeronautic Defence and Space Company) in Madrid and had an interview lined up.

Do you know what words I never ever want to see in my life again?

"We regret to inform you…"

Looking back at all the emails I had from the time, all I could remember reading was: "we regret to inform you…". And to top it up, the Masters interview didn't even bother to get back to me, even though I called and emailed several times.

Each rejection was that little bit more soul-destroying than the last one.

I spent the end of November and most of December in a state of depression, crying and stopping myself from crying.

Have you ever felt this way?

Simple errands such as going to the supermarket. A thought comes into your head and you can feel the pain in your throat and chest as all the muscles tense up because you just want to cry.

Your eyes start tearing up, and you try to blink as fast as you can to stop them from coming out. Breathing deeply to stop the water-works and do everything to think about something different and happy. Being in a public place and feeling like there's a spotlight on you, while you try to hide your face until you feel calmer and can continue with a smile.

This was a daily occurrence for me.

I wanted to tell someone how I felt, but I didn't feel I had the courage to. I'm not the type who is very open about their emotions, fortunately that has changed, and I am now more open, but I still find it difficult sometimes.

I tried to tell a friend. We were chatting online via messenger. He asked how I was doing, I said I wasn't ok and was annoyed about something, can't remember what. But he didn't engage in the conversation, so naturally I withdrew inwards. That was the end of me trying to open up about it to someone.

I was desperate for someone to notice and coax it out of me. I wanted someone to ask what was really going on and keep asking until my guard dropped. I wanted to tell someone how I was feeling, to let me cry and be angry and upset, without worrying about being judged or having to act like I had it all together.

As I write this, I can feel all those emotions I was feeling at the time coming up, the feeling of desperation for something to go right, the need for someone to understand what I was feeling, the uncertainty of everything, feeling lost - if I don't do this job, what do I do? The anger, frustration, and bitterness I felt. The wanting to just cry but constantly holding it back. The fact that I wasn't ready to be defeated.

I don't give up easily! Never have!

I was depressed but I didn't accept it. For me, to be depressed meant it was a sign of weakness, and I refused to be weak. So, I kept ignoring it.

The week before Christmas, my flatmate, Juan, asked if I would like to go shopping with him. I agreed as I had nothing better to do. The city center was full of people. Spaniards enjoying an evening dinner and drinks, people shopping at the Christmas markets. It was crowded everywhere. Lots of noise and merriment.

We went to Zara, the clothing shop. In the center of Zara there was an opening, so from every floor, you could see down to the ground floor. Juan wanted to try on some clothes. The men's department was on the fourth floor. While he was trying on clothes, I stood by the railings looking down.

I could feel the sadness and my throat and chest tightening. That need to cry was taking over me again.

Everything went quiet. There wasn't a single sound. It felt like time had frozen. Suddenly all I could see was me falling from the 4th floor where I was. Falling backward, so my arms and legs were just free in the air. The warm air flowing passed me as I felt like a cooling breeze on a hot summer day. Falling surrounded by white light. The brightness of the lights like the brightness of the sun.

My eyes closed and I felt calm and peaceful. The feeling of freedom and lightness flowing over me. Free of my situation. Free of my feelings. Free of everything. It was like a breath of fresh air. I could finally breathe.

This thought, that probably lasted seconds - a thought that I never, EVER thought I would ever have - was the thought that changed my whole life.

It was the thought of *what the fuck did I just think? How have I got to this point? I have nothing to lose. I have to go after what I want.*

I have always wanted to be an actor. I hadn't because it wasn't a proper job. But fuck it, what did I have to lose? The last 5 months I kept looking up acting schools. One kept coming up. I had even signed up to the mailing list. Why was I not doing that? After almost 6 years, why was I still chasing a job in an industry that didn't want me?

I wiped away any tears I had, blinked profusely to calm my eyes down, put on a smile and was a little shocked when Juan came back. I don't know how long that moment took, I had no concept of time. All I know is that was the beginning of a new part of my life.

The fear of going for something so different as acting was very much present. And just in case, I kept applying for engineering jobs. I still felt very down. I had my feedback call with Ford, I was so upset I couldn't really ask questions or speak because I knew I would just burst into tears. I stuck to one- word answers.

That Christmas I went home to my parents. I didn't want to go back to Madrid, but at the same time, I didn't want to stay in London. I wanted my mum to look after me. I didn't tell her how I was feel-ing, so she couldn't understand why I wasn't as happy as I would normally be. I didn't want to do family or friends' social get-togeth-ers. To put on a smile and got on with it, pretending to be ok and positive about what was really going on with me.

At the start of March, I found out I had an assessment center with Jaguar Land Rover. It worked out perfectly, that same week there was also a Weekend Acting Bootcamp with the school I was looking at. I knew straight away I had to sign up for the bootcamp.

The bootcamp was tough but felt amazing. I signed up to audition for the one - year acting school. However, this meant I would have to delay my flight back to Madrid and tell my parents about my choice to go for the acting. This was facing the first fear of going for something different. I wasn't sure they would accept it.

After some arguing and crying, my parents came to terms with it. And I started acting school in May 2012. It felt amazing. It felt very much like therapy. It brought up a lot of trapped emotions and brought me more in touch with my feelings, and to learn how to let go. You could say this was the start of my personal development journey.

The acting course was exactly what I needed to do. I finally started to feel myself again. I started to feel happy again. The thing I most wanted to do since I could remember, and I was finally doing it. I was performing on stage, in front of the camera. Getting that exhila-ration before going on stage. I was going to auditions, I had an agent, I was in shows. This is what I always wanted. I had more success with my acting career than I ever did with my engineering career.

From then everything started to fall into place. While I was doing my acting course, I got into Pilates. I had always used exercise as an outlet for my emotions. It was the thing that had kept me sane during university and during the years that followed. It made me feel better and happier.

The following year I qualified as an instructor. I wanted to bring that feel good factor of exercise to everyone. I wanted them to get that high from working out. I wanted them to have this for when things got stressful in life.

However, as happy as I was, I wasn't fully myself yet. Something was missing.

I discovered the Energy Alignment Method in 2016. I wasn't sure about it, but my intuition screamed at me to take the step...and so I did!

I loved how powerful it was at releasing trapped emotions and the massive difference it made, not only in my life but the life of others, and so I trained to be a mentor and help others with this method.

Being able to do the acting, the fitness, and mentoring was starting to really allow me to step into who I was. But there was one thing I hadn't dealt with.

It wasn't until I broke up with a boyfriend in 2017 that I realized I still wasn't fully embracing *me*. I had been with someone who pushed my boundaries and until then, I had let him. I had hidden part of me because he didn't approve of it. He felt threatened by it.

This was when I realized, I had to face the one thing I didn't want to. What happened in 2011 in Zara. I had brushed it aside. I hadn't really told anyone in detail about it.

There was no way I was going to do this alone. I couldn't talk about it; I couldn't even think about it. I arranged a session with one of the other mentors I had trained with. The session was hard, I cried a lot, there was a lot of emotion that needed to be released. Six years after it happened, I was finally working through it.

To be able to face it, talk about it, and let go of it was massive for me. I felt a huge load lift off me. I worked on this topic for the next few months and I truly started to feel like myself again. The confident, determined, optimistic, and happy Ceza.

I was in my power. I was unstoppable. I spoke about this event in my life in front of a room of business owners at a networking event. I was nervous as hell, but I knew it was important to share my story because we all have the power to change our lives around and get through difficult moments. We all have difficult times in our lives, and they are specific to our life journey, but we can choose to stay in that difficult situation or rise up above it. To step into who we are and be happy.

"There is a vitality, a life force, an energy, a quickening that is translated through you into action, and because there is only one of you in all time, this expression is unique. And if you block it, it will never exist through any other medium and will be lost."

— Martha Graham

Learning to let go of the bad things that have happened and learn to step into who you are and what makes you happy is so important. When you don't have to hide who you are or have to conform to what others want, it allows you to let go of the worry and stress that comes with being someone else. It brings a sense of freedom. You realize your own self-worth and the value you bring to the world. Your confidence shines through and there is nothing more appealing about a person than a confident person who knows their worth.

I love what I do now. This is not a job I ever expected to have, but I love doing it. I look forward to it every day. I have an amazing relationship with an amazing guy. My business is growing and shaping into what I'd like to take into the world. I live in a flat I love. None of this would have happened if I hadn't stepped into being truly me.

If there is anything I want to achieve with my work as a Relationship, Fitness & Energy Coach, it is this message: ***That you can be you, do amazing things, and have the life you want. The choice is all yours.***

Seeing my clients take control of their lives and fully stepping into themselves, into their power, choosing the life they will lead rather than being at its mercy, is the most amazing thing.

The first thing to do is notice where you are at. Are you hiding? Are you being someone else? If yes, why do you feel the need to hide and be someone else?

Are you enjoying life? Do you feel fulfilled? Are you happy?

If not, why not?

What will it take for you to be yourself and have the life you desire?

How you live your life and the decisions you make is your responsibility. No matter where you are in your life right now, you can improve it. The choice is yours.

3 Steps to Live Life on Your Terms

When I work with my coaching clients, these are 3 steps I get them to do. I will explain as we go why they are so important.

Step 1: What do you want?

Step 1 is all about getting really clear on what you desire. You can break this up into different areas, e.g. Relationship, Friendships, Family, Business/Work/Career, Health & Fitness, Money, etc.

Take yourself to a quiet room where you won't be disturbed (or even better go to a park, the beach, the forest, nature is always a great place to do this kind of work), get out a notebook, and write down exactly what you want for each area.

No thinking about what you *should* want.

No judgment of what you write.

No overthinking. Write from the heart.

It doesn't need to be perfect.

I just want you to start thinking and putting to paper your true desires.

We do this because sometimes we don't really know clearly what we want, and we end up going in different directions. When you are clear on what you want, your desires, your goals, it is so much easier to follow that one path. You are being truthful to yourself, which means you can stop chasing paths that don't work for you, or that make you unhappy.

When you state clearly what you want, it is easier to spot opportunities that will take you towards your goals and your wants. Your subconscious is geared to see those opportunities that will take you in the right direction.

The universe knows what you want as you've clearly and specifically stated it and it can bring those opportunities to you.

Step 2: Resistances

You have your list of what you want. Now I want you to read through your lists and see what thoughts, beliefs, emotions, patterns are coming up. Those things that are limiting your ability to reach your wants.

For example, you may want a relationship with a partner who adores you, supports you in your business ventures and is proud of you. But when you read that statement you have thoughts of "I will never meet a person like that", "This is impossible", "That person won't be attracted to me", "I only have relationships with men who are dismissive of me", "None of my relationships have been like this, so I don't believe it is possible", "I feel frustrated that I will never know this kind of love", etc.

These thoughts and feelings are the things stopping you from meeting that partner and relationship you desire. These are your resistances. Bringing these resistances to your awareness means you can start working on them.

A big part of my work with clients is identifying and releasing these resistances. I use the Energy Alignment Method with clients to release these resistances (learn more on my website, too big to explain here). I also ask them to journal what is coming up for them. To write how they feel, write their thoughts and beliefs coming up, write any patterns or habits they notice, to really explore why they feel this way.

Writing this out can be really powerful. It allows you to acknowledge the resistances and be consciously aware of them. This means it is easier to spot them coming up and stop them controlling you.

Step 3: Take action.

You know what you want.

You know what is stopping you.

Now you need to take action to change where you are at.

This doesn't have to be big actions. They can be small. For instance, when I was toying with the idea to quit engineering and go down the acting route, I would google acting schools. This was an action towards what I wanted. It took 6 months from the first time I googled it to when I actually booked the bootcamp, but each time it was reaffirming what I wanted and when the bootcamp opportunity came up, I booked it straight away.

You don't need to know all the actions you need to take, just do one thing.

If you want a relationship, sign up to a dating website.

If you want a new job, check what is available on job websites.

If you want to spend more time with friends, send a message or call a friend.

One step at a time. A baby step is still a step forward. No action means staying where you are.

You may find taking that action scary, especially if your resistances are coming up and trying to stop you. Breathe into it, visualize your wants and feel how it will be to have that goal, that life you want.

Tell yourself you let go of your fears and resistances. Take that action.

It is ok to be scared. Don't let the fear stop you. It really is the difference between staying where you are and getting to where you want to be.

Trust yourself.

ABOUT CEZA

Ceza Ouzounian is a Relationship, Fitness & Energy Coach, helping women be confident, get fit, and have amazing relationships through relationship coaching and fitness sessions. She is a qualified Pilates & Burlexercise Instructor, an accredited Energy Alignment Method Mentor, and a Beyond Wellbeing Lifestyle Prescriptions©  Provider. She is an inspirational Speaker and keen blogger. She is the Founder of Warrior In Training and the creator of Unleash Your Wonder Woman. Ceza knows the difference it can make when a woman steps into her power, believes in herself, and chooses to live a life on her terms, embracing her inner warrior.

WEBSITE: https://warriorintraining.co.uk
FACEBOOK GROUP: https://www.facebook.com/groups/WarriorInTrainingTribe

facebook.com/WarriorInTrainingwithCeza
instagram.com/warriorintrainingwithceza
linkedin.com/in/ceza-ouzounian

MONSTER IN ME

BY ELISE CLAYTON

'The feeling that cannot find its expression in tears may cause other organs to weep'.

— **HENRY MAUDSLEY**

When I think back now, anxiety has been part of my life for as long as I can remember.

As a child, I was labelled *shy*. I heard it so many times, that I thought that was what I was experiencing – shyness. That gut-wrenching feeling when anyone spoke to me and I had to respond. The sick feeling of embarrassment whenever any form of attention was drawn to me. Preferring to play alone instead of surrounded by other children. The dread of trying new things and breaking routine
- and the need for constant reassurance and praise from family and teachers that I was a 'good' girl.

I always felt different from other kids, because while they seemed to be having fun with friends, I felt like a bag of worries. My mind constantly questioning what was happening - what if people don't like me? What if I say or do something wrong - what will they think? What if something happens to my family? This little voice in my head spoke more than my actual voice. Sometimes I would even cover my ears in an attempt to silence it - but of course, it didn't work - because that voice was within me - there was no escaping.

Not to say that I didn't have a good childhood, because I did. I had wonderful support from my Mum and beloved grandparents, but I couldn't find the words to express what was happening to me inside. I didn't understand it. So, I kept it all in, put on a smile, and hoped and prayed that I would grow out of it and finally be *normal* like everyone else!

But over 20 years later this little cloud was still following me around – but now the voice was much stronger, louder, and more demanding. It told me daily how stupid I was, pathetic, a failure, that no one liked me, everyone could see my weakness and was laughing at me – and that I didn't deserve happiness because I was such a bad person.

This voice led me to spend my 20s living a life of pure destruction. After escaping a parent who reinforced my worst thoughts about myself, I left home and coasted from one bad relationship to the next. Excessive alcohol binges where I would drink until I blacked out, experimenting with drugs, constantly changing my appearance. I felt like my finger was always hovering over the self-destruct button. All in an effort to numb the pain of being me. But I never spoke about it. Who would understand? It seemed like everyone else was happy and coping with life, so why wasn't I?

Ironically, a few years later when I left university, I decided that all I needed to do was grow up and pull myself together. I found myself working in the world of PR and marketing – a people-facing business where communication and image is everything – the two things I loathed!

One day, as I sat across the table with six poker-faced strangers glaring at me, like I had done so many times before – scanning their faces as they half-heartedly listened to me pitching yet another crazy PR idea to help them promote their business, I realized that I had no idea what I was even saying. I was on autopilot, despising every second of the experience. I hated the sound of my own voice. I felt like a fraud. On the exterior, they saw a smartly dressed, professional, calm, confident woman, but on the inside was the same frightened little girl I had always been. I felt like I was dying, and at that moment, I wished I was.

What they couldn't see was my heart racing in my chest, my stomach sinking so badly that I had to fight the urge to retch, my palms sweating so much that I could barely click the mouse to move the presentation along. And what they couldn't hear was my own worst enemy, that little voice in my head which was screaming: "KEEP IT TOGETHER YOU FUCKING IDIOT!!!"

This was life for me on a daily basis for many years. I worked in agencies, where money was king, and people came second. Criticism was rife and backbiting was commonplace. I could never work enough hours or do too much. It was all-encompassing and eventually, it crippled me.

I felt like I was living someone else's life. I didn't know who I was, I just repeated the same pattern each day: Wake – panic, travel to work – panic, arrive at work – panic, leave work – panic, go to bed – panic. I barely ate for years. I rarely slept more than a few hours a night. I felt like I was in a bubble, hovering somewhere between the real world and the imagined, living a life of catastrophe with my overactive imagination sensing danger at every corner - afraid of it -

but also strangely wishing for it at the same time. Each day I would commute to work and imagine scenarios where the bus or train would crash. Sometimes I would sit and plan my escape route in great detail. Other times I just wished it would happen and imagined myself lying there, dying – a feeling of relief because at least then this would all be over.

But again, I told no one. I didn't want them to think that I couldn't cope. I didn't want them to think that I was weak. I knew it already - I didn't need confirmation from others.

I was desperately unhappy and was so worried that others would start to see it too - to catch a glimpse of the girl behind the smile, who was drowning. So, I tried all sorts of 'self-help' to keep it under control over the years – CBT, mediation, mindfulness. It would work for a while, but I always returned to the hole eventually – it was inevitable.

The breaking point came after a meeting with two clients with who I had been having a difficult relationship for months. I had worked tirelessly around the clock to get things right for them but for some reason they were never satisfied. The *chemistry* wasn't there according to them, and of course, I blamed myself. Because even after years of experience working in this world, I had no confidence in my ideas and always looked to others for validation. They knew it and at that moment I knew that they knew it. They saw through me. The deep, dark secret I thought I had been keeping all these years was out there in the open, plain as day. They saw past my smile and business suit. They saw the real me. They saw the little girl who didn't even know the first thing about believing in herself.

I sat and listened as they told me they had decided to pass the account to someone else, even though I had worked tirelessly for them for months trying desperately to get it right, meekly absorbing every criticism. All that time, energy, and anguish was now being thrown out. My eyes blurred with tears – but determined not to show my vulnerability I held them back. My legs shook, I thought I might faint (a common occurrence for me when panic took over), my mind filled with thoughts about how my boss would react. Sheer terror washed over me as I scanned my mind for a way to come back from this.

I couldn't see a fix, and I came away from that meeting wanting to end it all. Because after years of telling myself that I wasn't good enough, that I would never achieve what I wanted in life, that I was useless and stupid, and that everyone knew it – this was the final nail in the coffin. The confirmation that I had been avoiding for so many years had finally been handed to me, affirming all the bad things that I had been telling myself for so long.

That night I sat in my kitchen and finally let the tears flow. Tears that I had held back for so many years of holding it all together – keeping my secret – until I couldn't any longer. I sobbed in despair wishing it would just end. I wailed. I screamed. It felt like I was going mad. I was sure I needed medical help because I was losing my grip on reality. I felt a sharp pain in my head and my vision blurred. My heart was pounding so hard. And through my tears, I uttered the words: "I can't do this anymore. I am going to make myself chronically ill!"

And the mind is an incredible thing. It always does what it thinks you want it to do, and so it gave me exactly what I asked for.

Shortly after giving birth to my son, I began to feel ill. It began with me waking one morning feeling like I was wearing sunglasses. The vision in my one eye was dim and hazy. Instant panic and that familiar sense of fear and doom began to rise within me.

The doctors diagnosed me with a migraine - it lasted three weeks. When my vision finally returned, I noticed that bright colors seemed more muted, but I didn't question it - I was just relieved that I could see again!

Months of other strange symptoms followed. A constant pins and needles sensation - first in my arms, then in my legs. Numb patches on my face, a sensation of water trickling down my back, bouts of fatigue which came out of nowhere and knocked me out, confusion, difficulty with my speech, and flashing lights in my eyes followed. I was terrified.

Of course, I did what everyone does and shouldn't do – I googled my symptoms! Because that little catastrophic voice in my head told me that I had a brain tumor. It wanted me to know that the very thing I had wished for, for so long (an end to my existence), was finally happening. But now I had my son to think of. I couldn't leave this life now; my son needed me.

My search revealed everything from Lyme's disease to fibromyalgia. But the closest match seemed to be Multiple Sclerosis – a chronic disease which sees the immune system go into overdrive and attack the nervous system, causing the fibre which surrounds and protects the nerves to deteriorate in the brain and spinal cord - leading to all sorts of sensory symptoms and physical disabilities.

That word *disability* terrified me the most. And suddenly everywhere I looked there were tales of people ending up in wheelchairs months after being diagnosed, unable to feed or clothe themselves and completely reliant on carers or their family to look after them. I didn't want this to be me. I didn't want to be a burden on my family.

So, for the first time in a long time, I opened up and asked for help. I challenged the doctors who had dismissed me for months. I demanded more tests from the neurologist who told me it was just migraines. I began to ignore all the people who told me I was just tired because I had a young baby and was sleep deprived. I knew my body – and this wasn't right. Something was wrong and someone had to help me now. I wasn't going to be quiet any longer.

After three visits to the neurologist, he finally relented and I was offered an MRI to, and I quote, "put my mind at rest."

I waited anxiously as they sucked me into the giant bean can – thinking of all the things that could go wrong, all the illnesses that they could potentially diagnose. I began imagining the music I wanted played at my funeral and wondered whether I would be missed or if I would even be remembered after a while of being gone. Picturing my son growing up without me was too hard to bear. As my thoughts got darker and darker, my breathing quick-ened, my head began to float, and my heart raced.

I kept telling myself to think of my happy place, but I wasn't sure where that was any more. So, I closed my eyes and pretended the banging of the magnets was some sort of crazy techno tune – listening to the beat to keep me calm. I knew if I opened my eyes again, the claustrophobic environment would be too much. I made it through and hoped I would never have to experience it again, but a week later I was called back for another. The second time I was given a contrast injection. I had no idea why. No one told me anything.

An agonizing 4 weeks later I got the results: "possibly Multiple Sclerosis." Possibly?! I was taken in for a lumbar puncture to confirm the diagnosis. Large needles were injected into my spine to withdraw spinal fluid for testing, which left me with a week-long headache so excruciating that I had to spend it lying down.

I was called into the neurologist's office shortly after. I remember sitting in disbelief as he told me there was a 90% chance it was MS based on my tests results, and that only time would tell if I had another attack, or if this was an isolated incident.

As I stood up to leave, feeling shocked and stunned, wondering whether this was real or just another of my imagined catastrophes, I remember he hadn't referred to the issues I had been having with my eyes. He looked at his notes and said it was probably unrelated because it was just a three-hour migraine. I corrected him – three WEEKS – not three hours! There had been an error in my medical notes. He looked at me concerned and said, "Well Ms McDonald, yes, I can confirm it is MS, so now I'd like you to speak to one of our nurses to look at the treatment options."

I can't remember what happened next. It was like I was in a dream state. What I do know is that I left his office with a diagnosis that would change my life forever – feeling both a sense of terror and relief. Terror at what this would mean for me now – but relief at finally having a diagnosis and the realization that this was an end to living life in the world of work that had terrorized me for so long. At that moment, I realized just how much my career and anxiety had taken over my life. I had spent years lost in a haze of fear and loathing. So much so that I felt a strange sense of gratitude for a chronic condition which meant that I could finally be free of it!

Yet, I was still conflicted. The months that followed saw me flit between anger, despair, fear and disbelief. My head was filled with decisions to make on medications with horrific side effects, all with varying degrees of effectiveness. Injectables, intravenous infusions, pills. None of them guaranteed. MS is known as the snowflake disease which means it affects every person in different ways. And while they have theorized on what causes it – they don't have a definitive answer. But some research suggests that long-term stress, body trauma and a lack of vitamin D could be contributory factors. Suddenly it all made sense. I had deprived my body of its basic needs for so long, put it under so much strain, that now it was fighting back.

I opted for the strongest course of action: a twice a day pill which threatened all-over body flushing, gastroenteric infections, liver failure, lowered white blood counts, and hair loss. I braced myself for the worst. Each day I awoke with terror wondering what the day would bring – would the pills work? Would I be able to handle the side effects? If it did work, how long would it last? Because while the medications slow the progression of the disease – they don't stop it – but they would bide me time – time to come to terms with it, to learn to cope and to adapt my life.

Being diagnosed made me re-evaluate my life completely. At first my diagnosis was all-encompassing and all I thought of every hour of every day was MS. What did it mean for me? What did it mean for my family? What were the worst-case scenarios?

I knew I needed to be strong for my son and as time went on, I started to adjust to the new normal. I stopped crying at the knowl-edge that the symptoms I had would never go away as the damage was already done – and nothing would cure me. Gradually I stopped thinking about the *what ifs* and what the future held. I started to appreciate the days that I felt well. I stopped and surrendered to the pain and fatigue on the days when my body fought me.

As the acceptance process began, I realized that away from my son and my health issues, I had nothing else in my life. The anxiety that had plagued me for years and now this illness had turned me into a recluse. In anger, frustration, and shame I had locked myself away from the world. I needed a positive focus in my life. My son was just about to start nursery school and suddenly I was going to have time on my hands. I had no idea what I wanted to do; I just knew that I didn't want to go back to my previous work life!

After my diagnosis I joined several MS support groups on Facebook and like a signal from the universe, I came across a lady selling makeup through social media. I was fascinated by her confidence – doing live make up applications daily, talking about her struggles with MS and how the business was helping her. I had no idea about sales, or makeup, and the prospect of going live on Facebook terrified me. But I felt an instant affinity with her and shortly after, joined the company. It was a decision that would change everything for me. Because when I signed up for that little kit of makeup, I had no idea that it would set my life on a completely different course.

But it opened up a whole new world for me; it was a world of support where empowerment and self-improvement rule, and people come first! A land where women cheer each other on and build one another up, instead of tearing each other down.

It felt alien at first, especially after years of working in an every (wo)man for themself environment. But for once I really felt like I was a part of something. Before long I found myself doing things I never dreamed of – going live on Facebook, posting selfies on social media and doing crazy makeup transformations.

I threw myself into the world of self-development and became addicted to reading and learning again. I couldn't get enough.

My confidence soared as I read the works of Eckhart Tolle, Neale Donald Walsh, Michael Singer, and Marisa Peer, all preaching the same messages:

- You are not the sum of your thoughts.

- Your thoughts are NOT you.

- The imagined scenarios in your head are not real; they can't hurt you.

A huge lesson for me was understanding just how much the little voice in my head ruled my life. It put me down. It stopped me from doing things I wanted to do because it said I would fail. It told me not to speak up because people weren't interested in what I had to say.

I suddenly understood that this voice is what had been causing the feelings of dread and fear that I had been engulfed in for years. I could see it now for what it was, and I wasn't going to let it rule my life any longer. **In this realization, I set myself free.**

After years of feeling so alone and trapped in my own head, I began to read stories about people who had gone through similar situations and had overcome them to become successful. I started to believe that maybe I could do it too.

So I challenged myself daily – and saw just how badly I had been treating myself all these years. I began to feed my mind good thoughts, instead of bad ones. I stared into the mirror every day and repeated affirmations over and over: **I am strong, I am worthy, I am loved, I AM ENOUGH!** Until I started to believe it. I wrote it on mirrors, on my phone, and stuck the words on walls. I made time each day to meditate and clear the clutter in my mind. I began to feel within me how my thoughts triggered physical responses and emotions. I began to really see what was happening to me in a completely different way.

I learned that the issue at the core of everything that had been holding me back ultimately came down to one simple thing: The feeling that I wasn't enough. Not good enough, smart enough, pretty enough. I had always looked to others for approval – ever since I was a child. But I realized now that the only approval I ever needed was my own. And slowly I began to love and embrace myself – flaws and all! Over time, I finally started to see myself as the person I had always wanted to be – strong, happy, fun, confident.

Life felt so much better. Suddenly I felt profoundly grateful for everything I had. I began to experience a sense of joy at everyday things that I had taken for granted before. I started to let go of the guilt and regret that kept me returning to my past. The dark clouds that had plagued me for so long were lifting.

I rediscovered my life-long love of writing. I started blogging about the day-to-day battles I faced with anxiety and MS. I began to open up – me, the real one – not the one who hid behind a smile but was dying inside! I had found my voice and promised to never silence myself again.

As I shared, I heard more and more people join in and say, "I feel that way too." Suddenly I wasn't alone anymore, and I realized that so many of us sit and struggle, rather than speak up and ask for help, often to the detriment of our mental and physical wellbeing.

I drew people to me and into the business – advancing through the ranks by attracting ladies just like me who struggled with anxiety, confidence issues, and low self-esteem. I loved (and still do!) helping them start their businesses – but most of all I enjoyed watching them on their journeys. I love seeing them grow in confi-dence and self-belief. And I know that this is where my passion lies and what I need to do; I need to help others like me.

Watching them flourish made me realize that my life's purpose isn't to sit behind a desk pitching ideas to ungrateful clients. My mission now is to help others see that there is life beyond anxiety, job titles, and chronic health conditions – and it all starts with self-love. My goal each day is to feel joyful and proud of my achievements. I am living rather than enduring life now.

So, over the last year, I have embarked on a journey of self-healing and training to allow myself to grow and be in the best place I can be to help others. I have engrossed myself in learning about energy medicine, the relationship between the mind and the body, and the blueprint beliefs that we make as children which define who we are as adults. Absorbing teachings – becoming more spiritually aware – rediscovering my true self and surrendering to the challenges I face instead of stressing about it and trying to force an outcome, is how I spend my days now. By trusting that the universe has a plan for me, I have set myself free!

I trust my own inner guidance and intuition much more now and am kinder to myself. I feel so much happier for it. And best of all, four years on from my diagnosis, I feel well and haven't had any further relapses.

As I end this chapter, it seems very apt that I am about to start the next chapter in my life: I am training with Marisa Peer to be a Rapid Transformation Therapist - using a specialized form of hypnotherapy which helps people get to the core of what is holding them back in life. It helps them to get beyond the voice in their head and set themselves free from it, in order to live a life where they feel worthy, loveable, and enough! To walk the path they have always wanted, without doubt, or self-sabotage – and to feel genuinely happy.

After feeling lost for so long, I have finally found my passion. My mission now is to share my tale far and wide to encourage others to speak up, ask for help – and not feel ashamed about it, so that they never feel alone like I once did.

I am also on the path to my own self-healing from the physical and emotional traumas I have faced over the years. After reading count-less stories of how the body reacts to long term stress over time, I now understand that it can manifest itself in the form of illnesses and chronic conditions. It's the body's way of crying for help when the mind takes over. It is SO important to speak out!

But I realize now that MS came to me for many reasons:

- To force me to make changes in my life.

- To evaluate and realise what is truly important.

- To get me the help I so desperately needed all these years but couldn't voice.

- To learn to look after myself physically and mentally, so that I can help others who are struggling like I once was.

While I am thankful for all it has taught me, I have made the decision that MS has served its purpose in my life and it's time to move on now. And so, this chapter is just one of many as I begin to write my first book – The Monster in me – how I caused it, and how I cured it.

My biggest learnings and top tips for a more joyful life

1. If something is worrying you or causing anxiety, don't push it down and try to forget – allow yourself time to sit with it, consider how it's making you feel physically and emotionally, write it down, work through it one step at a time and ask for help if you need it. Because the more you resist, the longer it persists.

2. At times of crisis or challenge, allow yourself time to cry, scream, get angry - let it all out, then look for the lesson or the opportunity and move forward - stronger.

3. Don't be afraid to say no to people, or to walk away from relationships that continually drain you of energy and cause you pain. You are not obligated to anyone, except yourself.

4. One of the greatest causes of anxiety and depression is the words and pictures we create in our own minds. Be mindful of how you speak to yourself and ask, 'would you speak to a loved one this way?' If not, why would you speak to yourself this way? This is the first step to self-love.

5. Self-care isn't selfish – always allow yourself some 'me time' each day – even if it's just 15 minutes in the morning to exercise, read, meditate, journal – or to do anything you enjoy. I start each day with a short meditation and energy exercises which I learned from Donna Eden's YouTube channel. They are a great way to clear your head and energize you for the day.

ABOUT ELISE

After working in the world of PR and marketing for more than 15 years, Elise left to pursue her own online makeup and skincare business, following a diagnosis of Multiple Sclerosis. Through her work in network marketing, she discovered a true passion for helping women to build confidence and self-esteem, breaking the chains to what is holding them back, through self-  love, spiritual practice, and healing. She regularly blogs about her life experiences and day-to-day struggles with MS and anxiety on social media, and is currently training to be a Rapid Transformation Therapist using Marisa Peer's unique form of hypnotherapy which addresses the core issues holding people back in their lives – and sets them free to live the life they want.

FACEBOOK GROUP: https://www.facebook.com/groups/beyoutifulbellesVIP

facebook.com/eliseclayton24
instagram.com/el_beyoutifulbelles

YOUR LIFE, YOUR CHOICE
BY NADYA SIAPIN

Every time I thought about this project, only one year came to mind - but a bit of background first.

Reading through my story again, I realized it doesn't quite cover why I am the way I am.

So, to start at the beginning: I am the second oldest of 8 children. I helped raise the last 4 and began babysitting when I was 5. I was my mom's Right Hand, with a high expectation to remain that until I married.

Though I grew up in the US, I was raised in a super-conservative religious household. We are of Russian descent, and we cling tightly to all the old ways – even when they're no longer needed.

What kind of expectations?

That I would help my mom with everything that she needed: child rearing, cooking, baking, cleaning, milking the cow, fieldwork, gardening…You get the idea. Then one day, I would somehow meet a boy and get married and do it all again with my own kids.

Except, I didn't.

I honestly don't know why I didn't toe the line as far as wanting to get married is concerned.

Every girl I hung out with was obsessed with guys and marriage. Yeah, to a certain extent I was, too, but as I got older, I began to realize that marriage was something I expected rather than something I desired.

I *expected* to get married. I *expected* to have kids. I didn't really want either one.

Even into my early 20's, there was still the expectation that *some* boy, *somewhere* would actually look at me twice and miracle of miracles! I'd be married. Nothing in my life experiences led me to that belief. It was just ingrained by the community I was raised in. Everybody told me that's how it should be.

But the boys didn't. And I didn't get married.

I was part of a small group of girls who somehow didn't fulfill our parents' expectations and we were stuck trying to figure out what to do with our lives.

I had the added…benefit…of struggling to deal with both my father's sudden death in a car crash as well as my mother's decision that she was over his death in less than 3 months.

I eventually left home (which was Australia, we immigrated there in 2001) about 18 months after my dad died, and moved in with my grandfather in 2005 to take care of him for the last 3 years of his life.

I also got to be Grandpa's whipping girl.

He was in the early stages of dementia and would change his mind every other week about how he wanted to be cared for, though the rest of the family was in denial about his mental state. It meant I got 2 of my aunts yelling at me frequently, telling me I wasn't doing enough for Grandpa and I should be better. Gramps never told me anything directly, he complained to them and made it sound like I ignored him all the time.

Uncle Dave was way better, trying to give me time off, and being a lot gentler about asking me to change the way I took care of Grandpa. Though one time he asked me if I could be a little...nicer. I know I glared at him, and all that ran through my head was "He's still alive, isn't he? I haven't killed the old bastard yet! How much nicer do I have to be?!"

Let's just say that after all this, me and depression were on *really* good terms. I used to fantasize about suicide. I even knew exactly how I would go about it.

During this time, I did manage to figure out the next steps of my life. First, by seeing a naturopath who put me on a LOT of serotonin (the brain's happy drug) to balance me out, and second, by deciding to go to school.

I've been baking since I could see over the countertops. My mom would brag that I knew how to make bread when I was only 11. I figured that baking was the one thing I'd been doing most of my life that I didn't hate yet, so I might as well give it a go as a career.

Turned out, I'm a damn fine baker. I'm not much at making it look fancy, but if you want it presentable and delicious, I'm your girl. I had a job lined up as soon as I finished school, too, at a fine dining restaurant in Fresno.

With this bit of background, I hope you understand just how low I was later on. For me, rock bottom was a series of circumstances that piled up, and getting out of it seemed, at the time, like a natural set of choices. Did I want to help myself, or not? Did I want to feel better, or not?

Obviously, I did!

Except that, in the years since, I've seen a number of people who unconsciously answered those questions with a big, resounding No.

At the time, I worked at Woolworths – a chain grocery store in Australia – in the bakery department. This meant starting work anywhere between midnight and 3 am, and I had an hour's drive just to get to work.

I got to make 200-300 loaves of bread, and hundreds of rolls, every day. It was expected that eventually - sooner rather than later - I'd somehow do all of this within 8 hours and actually have time to take a break for lunch.

About three weeks in, I realized I'd been getting less and less sleep. Sleep turned into an elusive beast, coming for an hour here, an hour and a half there. Hours of tossing and turning, struggling to ignore the light shining around the gaps in my curtains.

I cried at the drop of a hat, or stormed around the house, raging that I couldn't sleep. Bags under my eyes, fuzzy mind, and my coordination started to suffer at work.

Do you know what happens when you're uncoordinated around hot pans and walk-in ovens? Pretty soon I had a collection of burns on my arms.

I'd seen a naturopath about my problems sleeping. They offered me something to help me relax. I think I got 2 hours of sleep that night. And that's about all it helped. I told the naturopath that the remedy wasn't helping and was informed I should just 'take more.'

You might be wondering why I didn't see a doctor. I didn't want to rely on a series of pills, to join the legions of people who take downers to go to sleep and uppers to wake up. Also, my body tends to either overreact to medication or not react at all. Cold medication will make me higher than a kite and pain medication with Panadeine doesn't work. So, I preferred seeing professionals who took the time to listen to me and tried to solve the problem, not the symptoms.

During this time, I met someone who had a huge impact on my life.

My mom drove me to a masseuse in the hopes that a good massage would relax me enough to sleep. During the massage, I chatted with Gail, a lovely woman with an interesting set of experiences under her belt.

Like many readers, I'm sure, I would daydream stories, stitched together from the many books I'd read. While I'd lay in bed, sleepless, one little original scene would run through my head, over and over, repeat forever. It drove me insane.

I mentioned it to Gail and asked her, 'How do I make this stop?!'

Her response? "Well, why don't you write it down? Get it out of your head!"

"But-but I don't write?"

"Maybe it's time you started. It doesn't have to be much, just get it out."

So, I decided to start at the beginning of the story. As soon as I thought it up. This one small interaction ended up having a huge impact on my life.

Over the next three weeks, I think I averaged 5-7 hours of sleep each week, culminating in a full 63 hours without sleep. I worked 2 shifts during those 63 sleepless hours. I didn't have a number to call to tell someone I really shouldn't be driving, much less working, in this condition.

* * *

The First Choice

This is where I had to make my first choice. My friend, who'd come sit with me and bring a movie to take my mind off my insomnia, told me about her naturopath, located near Adelaide. It was a fair drive from home, but pretty close to work, and Catherine said the woman would really *listen to me.*

Now, I could either choose to take a chance with a different naturopath - who would cost more than the last one - or I could keep plowing ahead and hope that somehow, things would clear up.

Albert Einstein once said that the definition of insanity is doing the same thing over and over and expecting a different result.

The choice was clear enough; not taking it would have been insane! I'll admit, at this point, I probably felt more insane than usual, but it's not like I was crazy.

So, I got Bronwen's number and made an appointment for the following week.

My experiences with Bronwen was vastly different from the previous naturopath. For a start, she listened to me talking for 5 minutes before she interrupted saying, "Okay, I can already tell your adrenaline levels are through the roof."

She handed me a bottle she'd pulled off the shelf with instructions to take 3, three times daily for the next week. After the first week, I could start reducing it.

That was the first night in 3 weeks I got a solid 8 hours of blissful sleep.

* * *

The Second Choice

I made sure to visit Bronwen regularly. At first once a week, then slowing to twice a month. Despite this, I continued to spiral downwards. Mild depression, mostly due to old memories surfacing, all compounded by a job I despised.

Don't get me wrong, I love baking. I find the process soothing, a creative outlet that had the additional benefit of being edible in the end. However, store bakeries are hell. Working a hundred miles an hour, crazy hours, high expectations for what you can accomplish, and being understaffed as a matter of course rather than an oddity. Add in a wheat intolerance that grew worse and worse...

To say I was still stressed would be an understatement.

Now came the second choice.

Should I stay in this super stressful environment that also happens to be the highest paying job I've ever had?

I'm sure I'd get used to it eventually. And if I left, what would I do next?

Finding this job had been difficult enough, and most other jobs available to me would be the exact same problems, simply different stores.

I want to say this all came to a head in June.

It was a Saturday night, and I was alone in the bakery.

I not only had to make all those loaves and rolls, but I also had to monitor the ovens, take the bread out of the pans, and put them onto cooling racks.

Either one is a full-time job, but on Saturday nights you got to do both.

Yippee.

I had a full-blown meltdown.

I cried as I rolled one rack out of the oven and another in. Wiped the tears so they wouldn't fall and contaminate the bread, and wailed my way through tipping loaves out of their pans, asking the air, heavy with the scent of fresh baked bread that I couldn't smell anymore, what I should do.

I had patches of skin on my arms in varying stages of healing from burns, hands so dry my skin could crack and bleed just from bending my fingers, and rashes up my arms from constant contact with wheat. And yet, I still considered staying in this job.

A small part of my brain was glad I was alone in the store, so no one could hear me cry.

Should I stay? Or should I try to find another, lesser paying job? What should I do?!

I didn't go straight home after work that day.

I wanted my dad, so I swung by the Smithfield Memorial Park. He was buried in a plot near the back.

I sat on the foot of his headstone, leaning back against it while my heart cracked, and I cried like a baby. I wanted clarity, focus, and most of all, I wanted him back. Over and over, I whispered, "Who am I? Who *am I*? Why am I even here?"

After all the tears, I finally reached an inner stillness. A little voice whispered, *"You are my daughter."*

As suddenly as that, it was time to leave. Everything would be all right. There would be a place for me when it was time.

Accepting Help

During this time, my sister had gotten an amazing opportunity. Using her Australian passport, she'd been able to get a temporary work visa for the UK.

Because it was a youth visa, you had to be under a certain age. I'd looked into it when I was 25, and the cut off age was 26. I didn't have the money necessary to get approval for a visa at that time, so I had to kiss that dream goodbye.

However, my sister decided to check it out. She asked the company helping her to check if the age requirement had changed. The cut off age was now 30. As long as you made it into the UK before your 31st birthday, you were good to go.

I'd just turned 30. A quick check showed I met every other criteria.

Once I decided to go, everything else flowed like water.

My sister became my biggest help at that time. I think I asked her a dozen times a week what she'd done, who she'd talked to, where she was heading in the UK.

I found a company to help me with my visa, gave a month's notice at the bakery, and began preparing.

My mood lightened as soon as I handed in my notice, too.

Life became a flurry of meetings, setting up everything necessary to process our information to get the visa. Banks, embassies, getting fingerprinted, the works.

I had also started planning a trip to the US for my cousin's wedding in August, making life even busier.

Now

A lot has happened in the years since.

I was living in the Scottish Highlands, working in an excellent little pub, by my 31st birthday.

I spent that birthday breaking in a new pair of hiking boots by heading out for a walk. I followed every trail I found the whole day. The weather was perfect, warm, but with a cool breeze and sunny blue skies.

I traveled around Europe for the first time, too. Hit up a bunch of different cities with a friend from England.

We went to Paris, France; Interlaken, Switzerland; Innsbruck, Austria; Prague, Czech Republic; Berlin, Germany; Copenhagen, Denmark; and Amsterdam, Netherlands.

After living and working in Scotland for a year, I was nearing the end of my work visa, so I decided to hit the road again, again with company.

My cousin came over to the UK, and we traveled together for 5 weeks.

We started in London, then went up into Scotland, all the way to Orkney. We came back down, stopping in the Lake District and finishing in Bath.

When she left, I traveled on my own for 2 weeks, hiking and camping. First in Dartmoor, then over to Cornwall, where I followed the Southwest Coastal Path. I broke my tent, bought a new one, and didn't sleep in a normal bed for the entire two weeks.

It was glorious.

After that, I headed back up to Scotland to meet another cousin, who traveled with me for 3 weeks.

We walked the West Highland Way, a trail from Glasgow to Fort William. It took us 6 days, and we had fantastic weather the whole time. Afterwards, we wandered over to the Isle of Skye to find the Fairy Pools. It poured the entire time on Skye.

But that's what traveling was.

I got WAY out of my comfort zone, and learned even more about myself, my preferences, and my capabilities.

After 3 weeks in Scotland, we parted ways, she went back home to Oregon, and I headed to Norway. I nearly fell off a cliff a couple of times, but Jotunheimen National Park was definitely worth the danger.

After that, I traveled to Brussels, in Belgium, where I made a friend for a few days and we explored the city together.

That became a theme, I would go to a city, explore some on my own, but also make a friend in the hostel and explore with them for a day or two.

I credit my time spent working as a server/bartender with my newfound ability to chat with people I had just met.

When I left Brussels, I went south, to Saint-Jean-Pied-de-Port, France.

There were some misadventures in Paris that led me to spend a night on a park bench in Bayonne. Don't worry, I didn't sleep and picked a well-lit bench. I only had 2 overly friendly guys I had to chase off.

I then spent a wonderful month walking the Camino de Santiago. For those who haven't heard of it, it's a pilgrimage trail that crosses

Spain. I walked the French Way, though I would love to go back and do the coastal path someday.

Walking there made me feel like anything was possible. Why? Because I'd wanted to do this trail ever since I read about it in a National Geographic magazine when I was 14-15. Except I always *knew* I'd never do it. And yet, suddenly here I was.

I was on the Camino for 28 nights, and for 23 of those nights, I slept in my tent. I walked, did a lot of thinking, and occasionally I would talk to other pilgrims on the Camino.

The greeting "Buen Camino!" is one I miss.

I did go 10 days without taking a shower, but that's because I wasn't willing to spend so much money just for a shower when I camped outside an albergue (hostel).

That trip didn't finish in Santiago de Compostela, as it does for so many. I continued on to Finisterre. I ended up going the traditional route and found the Atlantic Ocean, where I finally bathed. If you think that sounds awesome, or adventurous, it was freaking cold!

And absolutely worth it.

After El Camino, I adventured to Barcelona, with friends I made on the train. I ended my European trip with 2 glorious weeks in Italy. Naples, Pompeii, Rome, Pisa, and Venice.

It was time to go back home...This time I was different, confident I could take on the world.

But...that didn't happen.

* * *

Old Habits

I did have the confidence to take on vastly different work to what I was used to.

I ended up working for my brother-in-law. We subcontracted to NBN, Australia's internet network, installing internet cabling. I was one of 3 or 4 female cablers in all of Australia. Women installed telephones all the time, and internet modems, but very few did cable installation.

But I didn't go snorkeling like I wanted to. I didn't take my tent and head to the coast to camp every other weekend like I'd thought.

Instead, I babysat for my nieces and nephews, giving my siblings a chance to have an evening off. Or I'd stay at home and quietly melt because the heat was so intense that walking from one room to the other was enough to work up a sweat. Occasionally, I'd hang out with a friend or two. I don't have many people that I call friends, or who are willing to just *talk*.

However, it happened, my life became gray and stagnant. Again.

I fell back into my old habits, back into when I had no plans, no dreams, and no money. I went to work, came home, babysat kids. Life as Before the UK.

It's my own fault.

I had all these plans, and I didn't hold to them. Didn't ask around for ideas on how to safely keep car keys that aren't waterproof safe. Didn't take a close look at outdoor stores.

So, life began to slide past me once again.

The only real consolation I had was writing.

Remember Gail and her advice?

When Gail had suggested I write out that scene, I decided to figure out where it all began, and I started it as a proper story. By this time, I had around 200 pages, and a whole bunch of scenes in a couple notebooks.

I also wanted to travel full time, but I had absolutely no experience in any sort of remote work.

Writing seemed like something doable. Except I had no real experience. Then I realized! I'll start a blog.

Tons of people like to talk about how much money you can make blogging. Took a couple courses, followed the work to the best of my abilities.

Later on, I had to acknowledge how much of what I heard online is bullshit.

Do you know how many people out there say stuff like 'Do what you know,' and 'Find what you're an expert at?' I'm not really an expert at anything!

I eventually realized that they're nowhere near an expert either.

Ten minutes of Google taught me more than these so-called 'experts.'

There was still something else going through my mind... 'Should I stay, or should I go?

Should I really leave my nieces and nephews, this time for who knows how long?'

After all, the only thing I really wanted to do was to travel full time.

One day, while I was at my sister's house, I watched her dealing with her kids.

I thought about how my brother and sister-in-law handle their kids. I realized that, overall, they're doing a pretty damn good job at the whole kid thing. I mean, they didn't *need* me.

Did they want me around? Absolutely!

But I wasn't needed, which meant that I could free myself to be who *I* needed me to be.

This realization wasn't instantaneous. I'd gone back to Bronwen, the naturopath who took the holistic part of her job seriously. Not only did she balance out my nutrition, but she also gave me a series of exercises for clearing old, bad emotions.

I started by seeing her twice a month. After about 6 months, we went down to once a month.

I began feeling better, feeling like I could accomplish what I wanted in my life.

I also tried some advice she gave me.

Well, I say advice, it was more like a dare.

When I worried that I wasn't getting enough writing done, she challenged me to work on it for only 1 minute every day. That's it. Just 1 minute.

See, the way it goes is that if all you have time or brain power for is 1 minute, then you don't feel guilty, you don't beat yourself up for not meeting some huge goal. You got your minute! Yay!

Nine times out of 10, once you're set up to do that minute, you'll find the time and brain space to get in more, which is exactly what started happening to me once I tried it.

My guilt about my inability to write more often nearly disappeared. I stopped stressing about word counts, and just got some work done.

I managed to get a blog set up, very roughly, using this method. I had to Google *everything*.

I started writing it, and I'll tell you now, my earlier work is horrible. Like, painful for me to look at, but I leave it there so I can remind myself how far I've come.

Slowly, slowly, I changed old, bad habits, and tried to build new ones.

Life started looking better. I had finally begun doing things that would get me where I wanted to go.

The final thing I needed to get me fully moving towards a nomadic life happened in June.

Again, in June. WHY?

I threw a challenge out there to the Creator.

I needed final confirmation if I should stay or go, so I asked for a sign. If I were to stay, I would get a better job than the one I had. That's it. If I managed to find a better job, then that would be my sign to stay with my family.

What actually happened is that not only did I *not* find a better job, my current one completely dried up. Over the next 3 months, I got maybe 2 months' worth of work. Maybe.

I took that as my answer and started prepping to travel full time.

I sold what I could. Got rid of a bunch of things. Shipped all my books to my cousin in Oregon, and I left a single suitcase in Australia with a few things that I would eventually need when I decided to return. A few photos, some shoes, paperwork, and few clothes that I only ever wear in an Aussie summer.

I also began my goodbyes.

I have 7 siblings, 6 of them in Australia, 1 in New Zealand, and I've got 11 nieces and nephews. At the time, they ranged in age from 10 years to a few months.

I prepared to say goodbye to all of them, and I didn't know how long for.

I took my baby brother with me for the first country. We traveled to New Zealand, where we spent a week and a bit together. We started in Wellington, where I took him to the WETA Workshop as an early birthday present and we finished up in Hawke's Bay, where our sister lives. Then he went home, and I went traveling over both islands.

After New Zealand, it was off to the States – I tell you now, if I hadn't already bought that ticket I'd still be in New Zealand. The South Island is amazing! After a few months spent reconnecting with family and friends, I started up traveling again.

First Oregon, where I worked for an older lady who had a small organic garden.

Then Seattle, where I'd gotten a help exchange set up with a downtown hostel. I worked for 3 days a week and was right across from the Pike Place Market.

As great as the help exchanges are, they're not a great option when your funds are running low. I needed a job, soon. The others at the hostel were talking about seasonal work in Alaska. Seasonal work sounded awesome, so I asked where a good place was to look for it.

Coolworks.com was their reply.

As I checked through the website, taking note of the jobs that interested me, I got a fantastic offer for freelance writing. One that would set me up beautifully. Went through the application process, succeeded, and they said they'd get a hold of me soon.

I also applied for a job on the website, and I had one request for the Universe, the Creator. Each job would lead to a vastly different life, so I said, 'Wherever I'm meant to be, whatever I'm meant to do, that's the job I'll get.'

Well, I heard back from the Alaskan job (the only one I applied to) within 2 hours.

Without realizing it, I'd found the kind of job that suited me most. One that allowed me to explore.

Here's something funny… When I was in my 20s, hanging out with friends, we dreamed of traveling. Most of the girls talked about traveling to this city and that city for a few days here, a few days there. I dreamed of living in an area for several months to a year. Something that would allow me to thoroughly explore a region, get to know the little things that tourists never see, never know. Where are the best haunts? What's fun that very few people get to see and do?

After a year in Alaska, learning a rather large amount about the interior and north, I turned back to that website to find my next job, and my next location.

All the time, I kept writing.

When I finished the book, I printed it out and rewrote it from scratch. I opened up a fresh Word document and had the printout sitting next to me. Once I did that, I printed it out again and edited, and made the changes on my computer.

I've got a couple people reading the book right now while I figure out the bits and pieces, I need to finalize it and publish it.

Over the years I've been a baker, pastry cook, nursery laborer, restaurant server, bartender, cabler, reservations, guest services, horse-drawn carriage driver… and I'll only add to my collection of skills.

As the saying goes *Better a Jack-of-all-trades, master of none, than only a master of one.*

All of this started with a choice. Did I want to feel better, be better, or not?

I made a choice for my life, and I don't regret it one bit. I'm nowhere near done, either. Watch out, world. I'm coming!

Some of the best things I learned along the way have nothing to do with building a business. I actually don't have a business, which is just as well. Instead, my experiences were more about personal growth.

1. Learn how to be alone

Yup, you heard that right. Most folks are so concerned with what others think of them, and always reacting to the people around them that they never learn about themselves. To do that, you need to spend some quality time alone.

Go to a cafe by yourself. If that's too much, start by being home alone. Shut off technology. Read a book to get your mind working and see life from another perspective. I personally enjoy anything, and everything written by Terry Pratchett for a whole new view of life.

Then, once you're comfortable with that, go to the movies, to dinner, and for walks. If you're the type who likes to hike, go hiking. Find a safe trail, and camp for a night or two.

2. Make decisions

Have you ever had someone ask you what you want to do, or what you want to drink, and you just gave them a noncommittal answer? Just said, "Oh, whatever is easiest for you!" or "I really don't care, I'm not fussed."

Stop doing that!

You're constantly leaving decisions about your life in someone else's hands!

Making those small choices is a great way to learn how to choose, though. Maybe they'll ignore you, if they don't want to do the same thing as you, but you made a choice!

Good for you!

It also has wider reaching effects. Make a choice about where to go to eat. Decide what you want to read. You might not end up liking all your decisions, you might discover that you don't actually like doing something, but it will be YOUR choice. You can't blame someone else for that, anymore.

3. Let go of your past

Ah, this one is the hard one!

I needed a lot of outside help to do this one. I tried all those imagining things, writing letters and burning the letters…

Yeah, none of that worked.

It may work for you! But in my case, I needed a different path. I ended up doing a lot of exercises prescribed by Bronwen, and the only one I know the name of is EFT - Emotional Freedom Tapping.

Here's the main thing, though: if one thing doesn't work, find another! Don't give up, I know there's something out there that can help you! Maybe it's hypnosis, maybe it's traditional therapy, maybe you'll go a bit outlandish and find someone who does holistic naturopathy, or the Emotion Code.

Whatever it is, keep searching until you're able to let go of those old, negative emotions. They're not serving you anymore.

It's okay, you're safe, now. They helped you in the past, but their time is done.

ABOUT NADYA

Nadya Siapin is an avid traveler, writer, and blogger. She overcame humble, conservative beginnings to travel, and hopes to inspire others to reach beyond what they thought possible. Right now, she's working  random odd jobs - at the moment driving horse-drawn carriages - while shoveling the ideas out of her head and onto a computer in her spare time. She figures all of this will be useful someday to her stories. If you want to know more, head on over to:

WEBSITE: nadyasayre.wixsite.com/thestoryteller

UNAPOLOGETICALLY ME

BY JEN GAGNON

Have you ever woken up and wondered: *"How did I get here?"*

A little over 8 years ago now, that's exactly what happened to me! I woke up one morning and in that precise moment I remember not being able to recognize my own life. Suddenly I felt like the rug had been ripped from under my feet and I had lost all bearing on life. Well…to be honest, the rug had been tugged slowly, I just wasn't paying enough attention to notice it.

You see, the Universe has this way of giving you hints, over and over again and if you're not paying attention, you'll end up getting hit with an invisible 2X4 to really wake you up. I've gotten a few of those.

I digress…. back to that morning where I felt suddenly like my life was not my own. If I were being honest with myself, I knew I'd been feeling it coming on for a while, but completely ignored all the signs. When I looked in the mirror that morning, I could barely recognize the women staring back at me. I was unhappy, over-weight, and incredibly ungrateful for the life I was living.

To the outside world, I had it all: A husband, 3 beautiful and healthy children, a beautiful home, a thriving business, the freedom to travel the world, and yet all of that seemed so insignificant because I wasn't enjoying it. I wasn't making the most of it. I was what I call a negative Nelly! I was constantly seeing my glass half empty, never fully appreciating what was, because I was too busy stressing over what "should" be and more importantly what "wasn't"!

I grew up thinking that in order to succeed in life and have all of the nice things' money can buy, you had to work hard. I think most of us were raised thinking that success is measured by what you own, not who you are. I know I was. So, I spent most of my adult years chasing what I thought would bring me happiness and instead dug myself a big ole' hole of despair.

My anxiety and stress were through the roof. I found myself yelling all the time. I had never felt more alone and sadder. It wasn't anyone's fault or responsibility to make me happy, it was something that I needed to create, but I didn't know that at the time. It was easy to blame everything and everyone around me for my misery. It was easier to find all the excuses rather than creating a solution.

I had lost myself, completely in all my titles: mom, wife, employer, daughter, sister… In doing this I forgot who I was at my core and it would take me some time to rekindle the connection to self. I realized that I had three impressionable kiddos looking to me for guidance and I was a hot mess! I deeply desired to be someone who led by example, not just with words.

I started working out because I believed that if I was a certain size or weight that "that" was my key to happiness. Of course, it helped. I was working out and choosing better foods which made me feel better about myself. I was allowing my body to repair itself and remove some energetic blocks, but this was just the beginning; the work was far from done.

I was losing the weight and feeling a bit better, but the constant negativity wasn't going anywhere. Again, I kept focusing on when I'd get "there" not knowing where "there" actually was. Every time I'd lose a pound, I'd focus on the 10 left to go. Every time I'd hold for an extra second for my workout, I'd see the 50 left...Are you seeing the pattern here?

I kept hearing about these personal development books and thinking "those aren't for me", I'm living a normal life...or am I?!?!"

The first self-help book I picked up was by Wayne Dyer. -It was recommended to me by a friend- Ever since reading that first book, I became obsessed with all books relating to personal development. From Wayne Dyer to Louise Hay, Joe Dispenza, Deepak Chopra, Eckart Tolle, and Don Miguel Ruiz, the more I read, the more woo-woo it seemed!

I was reading the books hoping that something miraculous would happen from me laying my eyes on the words. It took me some time to finally realize that nothing was going to change until I took action and made the changes I desired. Nobody was coming to save me or hand happiness over on a silver platter. I had to come to the realization that happiness wasn't something that came with material things, it was a feeling that came from within, from nothingness. When you realize that the ultimate goal is to feel happy with your-self, by yourself. That happiness without the prerequisites, without anything...is the most powerful thing in the world. That one took a hell of a time to process. This was contrary to everything I had ever believed. Being happy is an inside job, it's created from nothing, yet it's everything. When I understood that I could be happy about anything and everything, life took on an entirely new sense.

I slowly started implementing the tools that were shared in these books and as I did, I began to notice changes in my life. Nothing around me felt like it was changing, but everything inside me was shifting. One day I noticed a Facebook post from an acquaintance about Marconic Chakra Unification and Quantum Recalibration. You have to understand that I had never really looked into energy healing. Hell, I thought it was all made up, really. But this time it was different, I was intrigued and felt called to learn more.

Two messages later and I had booked my sessions, I somehow knew that this was what I needed. Since that day in November 2016, my life has done a full 360! This was most definitely the catalyst for me, THE event that I can clearly see has changed my life.

Since that first day, I've never stopped working on me. The journey has shifted and changed along the way, but the one constant factor is that I show up each and every day, ready to do my best, for me and for those around me.

Learning and believing that I have incredible powers within me, learning to connect to me at Source, learning that I have all the answers inside of me has been an incredibly powerful epiphany. Knowing how to utilize those powers to my advantage is the other part of this journey. I've since become a certified Marconic Energy Healing practitioner because I know the powerful transformations this modality provides. The thing that I've come to realize is that it's not about what I'm given, it's not about what I learn, it's about what I choose to do with that knowledge.

I can have all the tools in the world, but if I don't do something with them, everything will remain the same; that realization took me years to fully wrap my head around.

I've come to understand that everything I thought to be true, or at least most of it, was in fact a lie. Society had taught me to view life in all of the wrong ways. Success isn't about material things or money; it's about the life you lead, and it's about the health and the happiness you experience during your time on this earth.

This journey hasn't been all rainbows and unicorns, as you'll hear a lot of people share. Just when I think I've learned a lesson; I feel another invisible 2X4 cracking on the side of my head. For a while, I wondered why I wasn't seeing the results I desired. I was doing all the work, showing up daily, connecting, meditating, being the best version of myself... all of what I thought I should be doing. The thing is, the shifts happen subtly, so subtly, in fact, we barely ever realized it's happening. It's like when a person is losing weight, they don't realize the amplitude of the loss as they see themselves each day in the mirror, but to someone who hasn't seen them in 6 months, the transformation is massive. Only a few months ago, I found myself, looking back and realizing how far I've come and... it's pretty mind-blowing to witness.

Since the beginning of this journey of mine, much has taken place. I thought I was living in alignment and then, in December of 2017, my husband had an unexpected, yet massive heart attack that nearly took his life, while on vacation. If that wasn't stressful enough, the day he came out of the hospital, my work bag (which I bring on all vacations) was stolen from our car. All of my work along with the back up for that work and my camera was in that bag. All of the things were gone! I don't have to tell you that I quickly spiraled down the rabbit hole until I recognized the lesson: LET THAT SHIT GO! Focus on what matters most right now.

I had to remember that first of all, nothing is mine in this life. Nothing! My husband is here having his own experience in this life. He has his lessons to learn, as do I. And this time, it was about letting go of what I couldn't control and appreciating each and every moment of life for the gift that it is. It was a lesson in knowing that material things can always be replaced and that stressing, crying, or screaming (all of which I did), would change nothing... It was a lesson in surrender and unconditional love. It was a lesson in letting go of my old beliefs and patterns, letting go of my fears, and trusting that I was always supported.

Let me tell you that when you're in the thick of the shit storm, it's really hard to keep an open mind and stay in your Zen. Luckily, I had the tools and more importantly the support system to do so. My Marconics mentor reminded me of who I am. She reminded me that everything is temporary, and that attachment is what hurts us most.

So many lessons! So many! These are lessons I get to master a little more each day. I don't believe I'll ever fully arrive, and I've learned to be ok with that. I've also learned through all of my experiences that I get to live a life I am in love with, without stress -or at least only a minimal amount - and doing what brings me the most joy.

I used to strive for something more in order to feel true happiness. I would think that if we lived in Costa Rica, then I would truly be happy (I'd still be happy there but am truly happy anywhere). Now I know that I create happiness wherever I am, regardless of anything around me. I've come to learn, and I continue to learn and put into practice that happiness is something I get to choose every moment of every day.

At first, I felt guilt for all those years of living a life that wasn't mine really, the one where I was trying to fit into the box: perfect mom, perfect wife, perfect employer, perfect daughter, perfect sister… damn, fitting into that tiny box with all of those things was tiring. I've let go of that guilt, I've let go of the shame around all the mistakes that I've made, because I know they were the stepping-stones to get me here. It's not a place, it's a state of being.

When you become at peace with your journey, at peace with who you are, your reality changes. I no longer want to be anybody else; I've spent enough time doing that. I want to be me, all of me. I have zero desire to be liked by all and I don't give a rat's ass about what others think of me, which is hard to believe coming from this recovering people pleaser! I strive to live my life aligned, appreciating each moment as if it were my last because I really don't know and neither do you. I've learned that I can see my glass half empty or half full, or I can lean into gratitude for having a glass at all, and that's what I choose.

This work I do carries through every aspect of my life. I no longer do business as I used to. I no longer allow stress and overwhelm to take over {most of the time}, I no longer measure my success by the same markers. I choose to do things in a way that feels aligned, in a way that feels authentic, and in which I choose to remain in my integrity.

When I began my journey, I thought that I had to figure it all out fast and get it right, immediately. Now, it's not about perfection in anything I do, it's about the being, it's about the enjoyment of the process of unbecoming everything that I'm not. It's about each step down the path that leads me home to me.

The biggest lessons this far, and I know there are more to come, is learning to love unconditionally myself first and those around me. When I can love people regardless of what is happening, when I can love them and still set boundaries, this is when the magic happens.

As I mentioned earlier, I have three impressionable children watching my every move, listening to my every word. The thing I desire most for them is to know how unique and magnificent they are. I deeply desire for them to see value in their health and happi-ness above all else. I want them to know that the field of possibili-ties is infinite and never let anyone tell them otherwise. I want them to grow up believing in themselves and knowing that in life there's no comparing because no two people are the same, we weren't meant to be.

My hope for them is that they know their value each and every day and that they learn at a young age what took me decades to understand. I know they'll learn their own lessons and I'm okay with that. I know that they are beautiful beings and that they aren't "mine", I do not own them. I trust that they will make the choices that they are meant to make for their own evolution, as did I. I trust that they will learn to forge their own path from the example I've set. I trust that they will lead the life that they were meant to and that they will create their own happiness each and every day.

I had to let go of the feeling that I own anything in this life and that was also something that took time. Heck, I'm still working at it! We tend to have this selfish way of making things and people our property.

As you can see, I've changed a lot! We all do! What would be the point if we didn't, right? When I look back at the version of me that began this journey, I remember how she felt. I speak in the third person because I'm no longer that version of me. She was sad, anxious, insecure, needy, judgmental, and just not so fun to be around! She judged herself and her shortcomings constantly. She strived to have more things to prove her worth. She believed money was the answer.

I know I am a lot more enjoyable to be around these days! I've come a long way and I know the road is not yet done. I've become more certain than ever of who I am and who I came here to be. I'm confident in my abilities and in the person that I am. I know my worth and remind myself every day that I do not need anyone to validate who I am or what I do. I understand that the Universe is supporting me even when I don't think it is. I know that life is happening for me in a beautiful way and I trust that every obstacle I perceive is there for my own growth and evolution and that it's something I get to be grateful for.

Every day that I wake up, I lean into gratitude for all that I am, for all that I'm becoming. I am grateful for another opportunity to do things differently, not better, different. I've come to grasp the concept of neutrality. Nothing is good or bad, those are qualitative words we've been taught by society. Everything just "is" and when you can come to that understanding you see life through a different lens.

Nothing is perfect, and some days I just want to say *fuck it*! I want to scream and cry and throw a tantrum…and sometimes I do. It never lasts exceedingly long because I know better, therefore I do better: I BE better. I have an awareness and a level of consciousness I've never had before. I live my life fully in each moment, feeling all of my feelings, and I mean ALL of them. I simply choose to let go of those that no longer serve me.

Part of the process that is engaged with Marconics healing is letting go of all the shit that no longer serves you; it can be a painful process. Painful doesn't mean that it isn't worth it. Kind of like when you work out and your muscles are sore as hell, you don't decide to give up, you know that the pain is simply more gain! Same here, the more I let go of the things, beliefs, people, situations that no longer serve me, the more I create space for all the wonderful things that do.

They say when one door closes, five doors open, right? I trust that with my entire being now. When I feel fear creeping up, because it does, I look it straight in the eye and deal with it. Fear will no longer control my life. Fear is really just something my mind creates to try and keep me playing small. I'm in the game for the win!

I do my best each day to make conscious choices, ones that are focused on health, happiness, and alignment because, in the end, those are truly the things that matter most! When I'm healthy and happy, and doing things from a place of alignment, everything becomes possible. I see too many people stuck where I used to be. Thinking they have time. Thinking that they'll enjoy life when they have all the money in their bank account. Thinking that they'll make time for their families when they reach the top. Thinking that they'll enjoy life when they finally retire. Thinking that they'll care for themselves once their empire is built.

Let me tell you because I've learned this one the hard way... You never know how much time you have, so always live as if it were your last day, always! Every night I ask myself, if I don't wake up tomorrow, will I have any regrets? Did I live fully today? Was I present for the people who matter the most? Was I conscious of my thoughts, my words, and my actions? Did I do things today that enriched my life?

I'm proud to say that most days, I'm pretty happy with my answers, but when I'm not, I make the conscious choice to change that. *I'm just a regular girl living an extraordinary life, because I choose to*. The way I do one thing in life is how I do all things! So, when I show up fully for me, I can then show up fully for my business and for my family.

All of this, the lessons, the growth, the expansion, the shifting. All of this is what brought the desire within me to help women do the same. Becoming a wellness mentor is one of the most fulfilling things. I know what it's like to be stuck, I was there. I know what it's like to feel lost, I was there. I know what it's like to not love the reflection looking back at you in the mirror, I've been there. I know what it's like to reach for every shiny object that promises results to crash and burn and find yourself at square one, over and over and over again, I've been there too! I know what it's like to constantly be wondering when the winds will change. I know what it's like to feel stressed, overwhelmed, and depressed all at the same time! My deepest desire is for every woman to create her own balance; mind, body, spirit, because that is how we create a life we are deeply in love with. That's how we let go of all that we are not and fall in love with all that we are. My goal isn't to teach women my way, but rather to take them as they are and help them, walk alongside them as they create their own with my help, support, and motivation. My client's success is in turn my success, because those women that start living life fully, in turn, lead the way for the youth around them to do the same, for the women around them to do the same. The ripple effect is never-ending, and that is something I do not take lightly.

My hope for you, reading this, is that you become so inspired that you decide to live fully, authentically, and in integrity with who you are, because there is no greater tragedy than having lived a life of a million deaths.

To you that is out there reading this and wondering how you get to start shifting and pivoting to create the life you deeply desire, I say this.

Create routines that you can stick to consistently. Don't try to do it all perfectly...perfection is for the birds. You get to focus on progress every day.

I'll share some of my non negotiables with you, in hopes that you will navigate your life and create your own.

1- Daily workouts (30 minutes minimum) Yoga, strength and conditioning, cardio

2- Daily journaling (even if it's only 5 minutes)

3- Daily gratitude practice. Before my feet hit the ground, I focus on 3-5 things I am grateful for and I carry that gratitude with me throughout the day.

4- Breath work & Meditation (10 minutes a day minimum)

5- Being aware of my thoughts, words and actions and shifting when I don't like what I'm seeing or feeling.

6- I repeat my affirmations 3 times while looking in the mirror.

If you do nothing other than this, I guarantee you'll see results, I guarantee it! You'll see every area of your life improve and you'll feel better for it.

Focus on creating more health, happiness and alignment in all that you do and watch your reality change!

Sending you all the love and wishing you a happy shift!

ABOUT JEN

Jen Gagnon is a certified Holistic Health Coach who helps her clients become crystal clear on their desires, remove toxicity and blocks from all areas of their lives, and finally start living a life of freedom. She combines her expertise in holistic health, mindset work, and energy healing to ensure her clients fully embody these shifts. Jen is a firm believer that in order to live your best life now, you need to align, mind, body and soul. Health, happiness and alignment are  the main focus of her work. She's certified through the Institute for Integrative Nutrition as well as a certified Advanced Marconic Energy Healing Practitioner, trained by the founder herself, Alison David-Bird (energy healing modality). Marconics is a powerful energy healing modality that allows the client to raise their vibration above the frequency of fear that has shackled them to their *story*. Jen has been a guest at several women's summits and featured in *Unchain Your Inner Strength Magazine* and podcast.

WEBSITE: www.jengagnon.rocks/
EMAIL: jen@jengagnon.rocks
She also writes regularly at www.jengagnon.rocks/blog

facebook.com/krazynfit

instagram.com/soulistic.vibes

pinterest.com/wholehealthwithjen

GIVE UP OR GET UP

BY CLAUDIA TINNIRELLO

Here I am again, in the place where it all began.

I'm writing my story while on holiday, sitting in the sunshine next to my husband, while my son is happily running around the garden, on the beautiful island of Sicily, my homeland.

I'm often asked by people why I left Italy to come to England, so I decided to share my story here.

I was born and raised in Sicily, in the South of Italy, by Sicilian parents, coming from a long generation of Sicilians.

Women in Sicily usually don't work. They leave their parents' home only once they get married. Their job is to look after the house and raise the children. They are not required to go to work and earn money. Sending the wife to work is a defeat to the husband, as this means his salary is not enough to feed the family.

And this story goes from generation to generation. My mum, aunties, cousins, grandmas all hold the 'Housewife' job title.

But I'm an exception. I'm the black sheep of the family. Independence and accountability are the most important things to me.

The truth is that I was deeply traumatized as a child by my primary school teacher.

If you have ever read the novel *Matilda* written by Roald Dahl in 1988, you will know the antagonist character of Miss Trunchbull. Miss Trunchbull is a fictional headmistress of a primary school, notorious for her brutal teaching discipline which mainly consisted of meting out psychological and physical punishments to her pupils.

Well, my primary school teacher didn't physically look like the fictional Miss Trunchbull but did act a lot like her.

She was an old-fashioned Sicilian lady, who outside of school hours, would spend her time at church preaching how to be a good catholic person. She used to always wear black or dark color clothes as a sign of respect for the loss of her loving husband who died something like 100 years before!

In my classroom, no one was allowed to play, have fun, laugh, or have anything colorful on our desk, like a colorful pencil sharpener or pencil case.

Punishing her pupils was one of the things she enjoyed the most, and her teaching style mainly consisted of slapping our faces, whip-ping our hands with wooden sticks, shouting at our ears, locking us in a dark room for hours, and even stinging our hands and fingers with sewing needles. These are just examples of her daily tortures.

Punishment is what I thought school was all about, and uncomfortable, fearful and dreadful place to be every day for 5 hours, from Monday to Saturday - yes, in Italy we do go to school on Saturdays too and only rest on Sundays.

For example, every single day I was petrified not to have done my homework correctly, because of fear of being shouted at, being humiliated, or most of all, being physically punished.

As you can imagine I spent the first 5 years of my school life in complete terror!

And my mum and dad could never understand why, every night, I cried and complained that I didn't want to go to school the following day, but they thought that I was exaggerating – after all, there is the misconception that children lie.

My sister, 3 years older than me, who went to the same school as myself, was always happy to go to school. Of course, she was! She never had Miss Trunchbull as her teacher.

And even after finishing 5 long painful years at primary school and moving into senior school, my belief was that all teachers were like Miss Trunchbull. I always kept my head down, did everything that was required to be a good pupil, a top student, and completed school with top marks. I even became the first in my family ever to get a university degree!

However, none of my primary school mates followed my same journey. Most of them abandoned school as soon as the law allowed them to and started working straight away – maybe they didn't want to face another teacher in their lives again?

For me, being top of the class was my defense mechanism, my survival mode.

Probably because of this, I've always felt the need to exceed and over-deliver, which also triggers the feeling of never being enough.

I don't know if I should thank my primary school teacher for making me want to always excel at school to avoid punishment, but

I've discovered that 'fear of authorities' has haunted me all my life. I've always feared being around teachers and bosses at work.

It took me several years to realize that that woman has psychologically scarred me for life, and the healing process is still taking a lifetime to complete.

I decided to spend my teenage years studying hard at school and university, rather than going to parties and chasing the boys.

Eventually, in the Summer of 2000, I met my husband Matteo during a Summer school holiday in England (UK). We were only teenagers when we met, and we have been together since.

Matteo is not Sicilian. He was born in Rome and grew up in mainland Italy. Before meeting him, I thought that all people in the world behaved like the Sicilians. After all, if you have never experienced anything outside your own four walls, you will never know what's out there. Matteo has been a great eye-opener for me and made me realize that there is more in the world, and the world is not just Sicily. He's always been supportive of me and has me become the person I am today.

In 2005 I graduated from the University of Palermo, in my hometown, and started to look for a job straight away. In Italy, it is extremely hard to find a job unless you have connections within the company. If you don't know anyone in the company you sent the application to, you have literally zero chances to even be considered for an interview.

Living in England has always been a dream of mine since I was 14. This is why I dedicated several years of my study life to learning English because I knew inside me that I would live here, in England, one day.

So, the opportunity suddenly came. A Sicilian friend of mine was working in an IT call center in England (and I'd like to specify, he is a guy, not a girl), and told me they were recruiting Italian agents who could speak Italian, English, and French.

So, following my job interview over the phone with the call center manager, I got the job and a room allocated to me in a shared accommodation with other call center colleagues.

I still remember the feeling of sickness in my stomach when I was at the airport waving goodbye to my parents. I was petrified! I was leaving home all alone for the first time ever, and for a long time - it was just 4 months!

So, my new life started on 1st March 2005 when I landed at Stansted airport and realized that my English wasn't as good as I thought it was. I even struggled to buy my one-way train ticket to Farnbor-ough, my final destination. That's when I realized that my English was excellent for the Italian standards, but not for the English standards.

I was in trouble! My job was purely a call center based, as such I had to answer the phone all day long offering technical support to English, French, and Italian speaking customers about IT things I didn't even understand in my own language!

At this point, I could have just given up or got up.

But I trained and trained, and cried and cried on a daily basis, wishing I could fly home for good and be back in my lovely pink bedroom I left back in Sicily, where I spent the first 23 years of my life, actually all my life.

But determination, and most of all pride, made me want to stay and go through the entire duration of my contract.

And just by giving this opportunity a chance, by staying, despite desperately missing home every day, I landed a new job within the same company, and then another one, and another one, which made my career progress in the marketing and digital department.

There was no going back now. There was no job waiting for me at home. This was my new home, my land of opportunities. Here I could get a job based on my experience and personality, and not just because someone would recommend me.

Also, Matteo followed me to the UK as soon as he completed his University degree in Italy in 2009. In July 2013 we got married and in December 2015 our beautiful baby boy Marco was born. Marco is truly our bundle of joy and it's a pleasure to see him growing into a confident little man every day.

And today, after 15 years, I'm still here in England. I'm a stronger woman, wife, and mum. I'm stronger than ever, and I consider myself a quite successful person in my field.

I worked as an employee for 14 years for big Corporates since arriving in the UK, mainly working in marketing and digital departments. However, I got made redundant four times in this period of time.

It is extremely hard to be told that by your boss that your job position is no longer required, and that they have to let you go. That really knocks your confidence down. The first time around I took it very personally, as I thought the company didn't want me as a person rather than as the job position, I was covering. So, I cried for an entire week; after all, I was only 24 years old, living alone in the UK, and had no support from anyone near me. I felt abandoned and rejected by the company I was working for.

However, I found a new job straight away, and then another, and so on; but I had to leave these jobs - not by my choice, but because my job was made redundant once again.

Thinking back, and to be honest with myself, I was never feeling fulfilled by all those jobs. I was purely working for money, only looking forward to the weekends, my time of freedom. I was stuck Monday to Friday, from 9 am to 5 pm. I was starting to feel trapped in an office building for far too many hours in my day, doing a job that didn't fully satisfy me, and mainly working hard to make my superiors richer.

So when the very last redundancy hit me in November 2019, I decided that enough was enough and it was time to start taking control of my life, rather than letting another HR person tell me that my service was no longer required. So, I abandoned the corporate world and set up my own company.

Today I am the proud CEO and founder of Sophisticated Cloud Limited. Our mission is to help a million people to be heard and seen by having a robust online presence and embracing public speaking. We achieve this by offering our clients access to our years of experience in web design, online marketing, and public speaking. We specialize in creating affordable websites that look great, work great, and are designed with our client's target audience in mind. And as well as helping our clients share their voice online, we also help them embrace public speaking - an essential skill to help grow anyone's business.

I can now virtually work anywhere in the world, provided I have access to my laptop and internet connection. I'm free to choose the hours I want to work, the people I want to work with, and the projects I want to embark on.

I no longer have to ask permission from my boss to take a day off or time for annual leave, because I am the boss now, and I absolutely love it! I am a completely independent woman now. This is what freedom is for me.

I know it takes guts to start your own business and give up on the security of a stable salary every month, but I also have to give credit to my training as a Toastmasters International public speaker.

Toastmasters International is a non-profit educational organization that teaches public speaking and leadership skills through a world-wide network of clubs. Since 1924, Toastmasters International has helped people from diverse backgrounds become more confident speakers, communicators, and leaders.

Before joining Toastmasters, I dreaded public speaking so badly that I was petrified of even saying my name in front of a crowd. So, when someone recommended, I attend a Toastmaster meeting, I was intrigued. I went to a meeting and loved the safe environment. No one judges you. They teach. You learn. I had this positive energy coming towards me. I loved standing up in front of people!

Within seven months of my first meeting, I was elected Vice President of Public Relations. Today I'm the proud President of Toast-master International Basingstoke Speakers Club. Being the President of an English speaker club makes me immensely proud, considering that when I arrived in the UK my English was a real disaster. This goes to show that when you work hard on improving and polishing your skills you can really reach the sky!

Toastmaster has seriously helped me gain the confidence to put one foot in front of the other to get me wherever I wanted to be, and now I know that the world is my oyster.

Throughout my life journey, there have been quite a few moments when I was ready to give up and go back home. After all, I was just a girl, and girls should stay at home. This is what I've been told by society all my life.

But I don't regret a single moment, the struggles and pain I've been through. And most of all, I couldn't imagine my life as a traditional Sicilian wife.

So, my message to you all is, don't let society put a label on you. You can be whatever you wish you to be. You will always have a choice in life, you can give up or get up.

And every day I choose to get up.

3 tips to help you manage your nerves and the fear of public speaking

Public speaking is not that difficult really. Although before climbing the steps of the podium to give a talk, many of us have to face our own personal insecurities.

Some people feel insecure about the way they look. They worry that they're too old, too young, too fat, or too thin. They don't like their hair, their nose, or their teeth. So, they feel doubly exposed when they stand up to speak in public.

It may be worth remembering that many people in the audience aren't particularly in love with their faces or their bodies either and aren't judging you nearly as much as you think you are.

So, there you are, standing up in front of a group of people. Your muscles start to shake, you feel sick, you can't remember a word, your mouth goes dry, you can't swallow, and your voice stops working. Not great, is it?

Why does this happen?

Back in the days when we were living in caves and being attacked by wild animals, our bodies sent panic alarms to the neural path-ways in the oldest part of the brain, called the amygdala. This is the so-called 'fight or flight' response.

The brain is often unable to judge the severity of danger and can respond to fear disproportionally. So, whether we are being attacked by a wild animal or facing fifty colleagues at work, the brain sends signals along those ancient neural pathways.

These signals, identified as the seven-fight or flight responses, tell us either to fight or to run.

The seven-fight or flight responses:

1. At times of life-threatening danger, the brain downgrades the importance of its own functions. Running away is far more important than thinking about running away. So, the brain sends a message to the heart, to increase the blood flow so that it can send oxygen and adrenalin via the blood supply to our legs and arms to fight or to run. Therefore, we have less blood running in the brain, which can result in forgetting our words or, as in the worst-case scenario, actually fainting!

People that have done heroic acts in dangerous situations often say afterward, 'I don't remember much about it – it was all just a blur.'

2. A message is then sent to the lungs. We'll need more oxygen if we are to fight or run, so we'll need to increase our breathing rate. But as we're giving a speech and not using up this extra oxygen, we can end up hyperventilating, making us feel light-headed.

3. The brain sends adrenaline to our eyes, so we can find an escape route. We can often see a speaker's eyes darting around the room wildly or looking slightly scared.

4. As there's a small chance the 'wild animal' hasn't seen us, the brain turns off our voice box to protect us from being detected. So now we can't speak.

5. We don't want to choke on our own saliva as we run, so the brain stops producing saliva. That's why we often have a dry throat and mouth.

6. The brain sends signals to draw blood away from the stomach as there's no time to digest food. The blood is now needed to give your muscles extra firepower. This can leave us feeling slightly sick – not a great prospect for after dinner speakers!

7. You're standing up in front of your audience, and the body is sending ancient chemical signals urging your body to run. But you are about to give a speech and you can't run. So, the muscles become overloaded with oxygen and adrenalin and they simply cannot stand still any longer. This is the physiological reason why we shake.

What we, as speakers, have to do is to learn how to cope with these responses. We have to learn how to use all that adrenalin to our advantage.

TIP #1 - SQUEEZE YOUR GLUTES

It is almost physically impossible to shake if you squeeze your thighs, not squeezing them with your hand, but by tightening the muscles themselves. I promise you it will stop you from shaking.

In the fight or flight mode, by squeezing our thigh muscles the body thinks we are moving and stops producing adrenaline. So, miraculously, we will stop shaking.

Also, the more we squeeze our muscles, the more we are sending blood back up to the brain. So now we are less likely to feel lightheaded or to forget our words.

TIP #2 - PUSH A WALL

Stand and face a wall. Place both hands on the wall about shoulder height and push really hard for a few seconds, as if you were trying to push the wall a couple of meters in the direction you are pushing. This is a great exercise for releasing tension in the upper chest. It frees your voice and helps relax any nervous tension.

TIP #3 - SLOWING DOWN YOUR HEART RATE

This is an exercise that you can do even when people are watching you.

Breathe in through your nose slowly for a count of three. Then breathe out through your nose for a count of three. Repeat this three times. That should take a total of 18 seconds. In that time, you will have significantly lowered your heart rate.

ABOUT CLAUDIA

Claudia Tinnirello is the CEO and founder of Sophisticated Cloud. She is a professional SquareSpace Web Designer, UX expert, former cookery chef, and enthusiastic public speaker. Originally from
Italy, Sicily, she has lived in England since 2005. Following her fourth redundancy at work, she decided to set up her own Web Design business which she absolutely loves. She works with small businesses that want to build beautiful one of a kind responsive website, that are SEO optimized and compatible on all screens and devices - desktop, tablet, and mobile phones. She is currently the President of the Toastmasters International Basingstoke Speakers Club. Not being an English native speaker, she understands the struggles of overcoming judgments and fear of making mistakes when speaking a foreign language. She has discovered ways of becoming a better and confident public speaker by sharing her voice in many different ways, from speaking opportunities to building websites, to cooking food. Her mission is to help a million people to be heard and seen by having a robust online presence and embracing public speaking.

WEBSITE: www.sophisticatedcloud.com
EMAIL: claudia@sophisticatedcloud.com

f facebook.com/claudiatinnirellowebdesign

⊙ instagram.com/claudiatinnirello_webdesign

in linkedin.com/in/claudia-tinnirello

THE REIGNITED WOMAN

BY JOYCE HARDIE

Getting sick was the best thing that ever happened to me!

That sounds totally like a ridiculous thing to say, and at the time I didn't think it was good at all, but it has led to so many positive things.

Before I became unwell, I led a normal life. I lived with my husband and teenage daughter and I had a good job which I thought I would be in till I retired. We had the normal fights and arguments but in general, life was good, we went on great holidays, my daughter went to private school and we had a lot to be thankful for.

Don't get me wrong life also had its downsides. I was on call 24/7, 365 days a year, I travelled back and forth to London every week, I was going through menopause and had a hormonal teenager to deal with! Managing the menopause is bad enough, dealing with a hormonal teenager at the same time is like living in a war zone. I'm sure that's why my husband took a job in Dubai! But I'm getting ahead of myself.

Back in January 2011, I started waking up with pain in my hands and I started cracking my joints, a practice I hate, to try and ease the pain. I put it all down to my age and thought that it was arthritis or rheumatics. But then I started getting pins and needles in my feet, normally when I was at church, so I put that down to the chairs in the sanctuary. By the time July came, I had pain all over my body which I couldn't justify to myself, so I made an appointment with my GP.

Her reaction freaked me out!

She asked if I had private medical insurance because if I could, I should see a specialist neurologist right away. Private medical insurance was one of the perks I had at work, so the GP made the referral and I saw the consultant within a few days. He did loads of tests but couldn't find anything wrong, so he sent me to a rheumatologist who did loads of tests but couldn't find anything wrong, so he sent me to an orthopedic consultant who did loads of tests and...you've guessed it. He didn't find anything wrong.

It was only after many more tests that I was referred to a Cardiologist, who did tests and couldn't find anything wrong, but he said, "I think you have Fibromyalgia." After 11 months of being poked, prodded, and blood tests, I finally had a diagnosis. I have fibromyalgia.

During those 11 months, life hadn't stopped. I was prescribed medication and kept working as if nothing had happened. Commuting between Glasgow and London, parenting a stroppy teenager, housework, shopping, and all the other things that make up everyday life.

Early in 2012, my husband was offered his dream job.

The problem? It was in Dubai.

Now, I know too many people where that wouldn't be a problem, but we had a lot to talk about. Would I be able to get work in Dubai? What about our daughter, who was just about to sit her stan-dard grades and had two years left at school?

So, the decision was made, Alex would go to Dubai and I would stay at home with our daughter to let her finish school. We agreed to revisit the situation when Kirstie went to University.

And so, for a year thing progressed as before, with the exception that we travelled to Dubai whenever the school holidays permitted. It became our home away from home, but better because we made every effort to ensure the time we spent together as a family was quality time. We visited attractions, lazed by the pool, dined out, and invited friends to come and stay with us. It was as good as it could be.

Till… a Sunday morning in June 2013 when I couldn't get out of bed. Every part of my body ached, and it was impossible to put my feet on the floor and stand up, so I pulled the duvet over my head and decided to try again tomorrow. Except tomorrow wasn't any different, nor the next day, nor the next day. A visit from the doctor confirmed that I had taken a virus which, when it was combined with my existing condition, had absolutely floored me.

That was the end of my life as I knew it!

I could no longer work, and as a result, I parted ways with my employer eight months later. That process has been discussed else-where so I won't go over it again, suffice to say that it was handled very badly, which culminated in someone stealing the collection that the staff had contributed to for me. What kind of person steals money from the sick?

That was the start of a really bad year. In addition to losing my job, I continued to struggle with my health. I had no income and no obvious way of getting one, as I never knew when I would be able to work and when I couldn't. My dad passed away and my daughter moved out to go to University.

October 2014 found me home alone, rattling about in a 4- bedroom house and twiddling my thumbs. I was angry! I was angry with my previous employer, I was angry that I couldn't move to Dubai because I couldn't get health insurance, I was angry that my husband didn't come home, and I blamed myself for the loss of income and what that meant for us as a family.

I desperately needed support and comfort. Yes, I was feeling sorry for myself, so I tried to find comfort at the bottom of a wine bottle. A glass of wine every other night turned into a glass or two every night, and then a bottle a night. It's not something I'm proud of but it was something that happened almost without me noticing it.

I couldn't tell anyone what was happening as I was ashamed of what I was doing. I knew I needed to snap out of it, or it would get totally out of control, but it's a bit like dieting. We all know what to do but it's never that easy when we try.

One of the things that hit me hard was loneliness. According to the Office for National Statistics, Britain is the "loneliness capital of Europe," but when you're lonely and isolated you don't know anyone else who is lonely. Everyone you know is happy and surrounded by people, magazines show couples having a great time, and even on TV, you don't see anyone sitting at home with loneli-ness eating into their soul.

"The greatest suffering is being lonely, feeling unloved, just having no one," Mother Teresa wrote. Loneliness is the leprosy of the 21st century, eating away at its victims and repelling those who encounter it.

As your loneliness increases, your confidence decreases till I didn't want to go out. I didn't want to mix with people who I was convinced were only seeing me because they felt sorry for me. Nothing made me feel better, I always felt as if I was on the outside just being tolerated. Don't get me wrong I still had family living close by but that didn't change how I felt.

During this time, I had set up my first business, a facilities management business, doing exactly what I had done in the corporate world. And just the same as the corporate world I put my profes-sional mask on every time I walked out the front door. I told everyone that everything was going well when it wasn't. I worked long days and while I got some work it was never going to go anywhere.

My health continued to deteriorate, my feeling of loneliness and isolation increased. I decided to change the business to suit my health and decided to focus on producing business documents for companies. The logic was that I could do this when my health permitted, and I didn't need to leave the house to do it! Great plan for an introvert who was extremely lonely!

I joined an online freelance site to try and get money. The information from the clients was limited, and I spent long hours trying to set up other people's businesses for truly little in return.

Around that time an acquaintance, who is now a good friend, invited me for a coffee, and for whatever reason, I opened up and told her about the drinking. I didn't confess to being lonely! I blamed everything else, my health, my husband being away, and the difficulties of a long-distance relationship but still kept the focus away from me and what I was really feeling.

I have grown up believing that I wasn't good enough, not pretty enough, not smart enough, not anything, and that was a belief that coloured everything I did. Who would want to be friends with someone like me? Who would want to spend time with me when they had their own families?

Loneliness, low self- esteem, and deteriorating health all worked for hand in hand, creating a new belief system which identified who I was. A poor specimen of humanity in a long-distance relationship leading a separate life from the love of my life.

Then one day I woke up and decided I couldn't do it anymore. I couldn't stand the loneliness, the lack of friendship, my self-destructive lack of self-esteem, the mounting debt, and my deteriorating health.

It was over, I couldn't do it anymore!

I knew I needed help but didn't know where to find it! I searched online but all I found was women half my age and with absolutely no life experience. What could they do to support a menopausal, lonely, middle-aged woman with a chronic illness and no self-esteem?!

But help always comes when you need it the most. A friend was chatting one day about a counsellor that they had referred someone to, so I asked for the details suggesting it was for someone I knew. One thing women are great at is wearing a mask and hiding the things that are really important to them, so I was never going to tell them it was for me.

I made the call, but luckily no one answered. I debated whether or not I should leave a message, and before my courage failed, I left my name and number. I was actually hoping that she wouldn't call me back, but she did.

I had become so proficient at wearing a mask that I never spoke about anything that was important, was so alien to me, and the thought of opening up to a stranger absolutely freaked me out. I remember the first couple of sessions. I sat hiding behind my scarf, saying as little as possible for every answer. But as time went on, I started to open up and talk about everything.

We talked about my health, work past and present, my marriage, my low self-esteem (I went for a long time!). There were lots of tears but also lots of revelations as I started to unwind. We went over why I felt the way I did. Why I blamed myself for getting sick, why my business failed because I didn't believe in my abilities and the biggest revelation was why I was letting my marriage drift rather than fighting for what I wanted.

It wasn't an easy process but identifying how little I thought of myself was the hardest thing to get my head around. My fear of saying the wrong thing and causing conflict made me say nothing and let others make my decisions even if it wasn't what I wanted. Taking off the mask that I had worn all my life was painful and left me totally vulnerable. Don't get me wrong, I still wear it sometimes but that is a deliberate choice I make when talking to certain people.

Removing the mask left me feeling exposed. I was sure that I would be seen for what I was, not good enough.

I have never felt good enough. At school, I passed exams, but I wasn't amongst the brightest in my year. I had to work hard but it was never good enough - not for my teachers and not at home either. I wasn't pretty, I wore braces at a time when that was differ-ent, I was plain and certainly not the centre of attraction. I never had exciting stories to share about boys, I never watched the right programmes on TV, I had nothing to say.

To be honest I still don't watch the right TV programmes because now, as then, I would rather read a book than watch TV. The differ-ence is that now I'm happy to say that out loud.

I don't keep in touch with anyone from school, except for Alex, who was the year above me and who I started to date in my final year. I felt so bad about myself that I couldn't believe that there was a big positive statement staring me in the face, my marriage! Alex and I have been together for 43 years and have been married for 34 years. That is quite an achievement. No, it hasn't always been plain sailing, but we have managed to work our way through the bad times.

Another positive that came out of seeing a counsellor is that I started to talk to Alex about how I really felt about myself. He couldn't believe it; he had no idea how insecure I was. It took time because no matter how hard you try you cannot break 50 years of habit in one night, but we are now communicating again rather than just talking!

I've never had a lot of friends because I (felt I) had nothing to talk about and because I wouldn't let anyone in. I'm not saying I have lots of friends now because I don't, and there are times when I have to stop myself wondering why some people would want to be friends with me, but I am getting better. They say that when things reach rock bottom, the people that are there for you are true friends, and I know that is true.

I was recently rushed to hospital with a serious health scare. I have blood clots in my lung, and it was apparent both at the time and since who has been there for me and it wasn't the people that I expected! Some people like to think they are friends, but it needs to be on their terms and that is not good enough.

The biggest change since all of this happened is that I've set up a new business called The Reignited Woman, working with women over 40. Why did I do this? To be there for women like me, who feel they are not good enough, who are lonely, who don't have someone there for them when times are hard.

I want to be there for others in the same way that my counsellor and a friend were there for me. I'm not a counsellor, and never want to be one. I want to help women move forward and not backwards.

The crazy thing about this new business is that it has taken me back to where I started. Forty years ago, I graduated with a Social Science degree and a desire to become a social worker or something similar. But when I graduated, I was too young to do the relevant course, so I had to take a year out. It was one of those things - I couldn't get a job in my preferred sector because I wasn't qualified, and I couldn't get qualified because I was too young!

The only action available was to take any job I could get and that was the worst job ever, working in accounts payable for a large department store. I hate numbers, I hate sitting doing the same thing hour after hour. There was no way it was going to last, and it didn't.

I was moved to another department to project manage the launch of a new credit card, which led me into the property industry, and the job that I did for 34 years, Facilities Management. I often felt that facilities management was a bit like social work simply because everyone told you what was wrong and expected you to fix it. I loved my job and thought I would be there till I retired, but my health got in the way!

I now love what I do and have built programmes and training around the problems that I have faced, loneliness, low self-esteem and health issues as well as other areas of my life. I can relate to what women are going through, and if I hadn't found the right person to talk to my life would not be the amazing life I have today.

I owe everything I am today to two amazing women and to getting sick!

You are never too old to learn something new.

Do one thing that scares you every day.

Try to think about what's missing in your life. The more clearly you know what is missing the easier you will find a solution

Healthy aging means continually reinventing yourself as you pass through landmark ages such as 40, 50, 60, 70, 80 and beyond. It means finding new things you enjoy, learning to adapt to change, staying physically and socially active, and feeling connected to your community and loved ones

Take Pride in Your Workspace. Whether your space is a laptop-friendly desk or behind a cash register, make cleanliness and organization a priority for where you spend the majority of your time. It can actually be fun to work when your space is an extension of your personality, giving you a comfortable place to concentrate and perform. Doing this will also keep you from losing important things (like money).

Hobbies bring a sense of fun and freedom to life that can help to minimize the impact of chronic stress because it provides great insight into your personality, creativity and passion.

ABOUT JOYCE

Joyce Hardie is married with a grown-up daughter. At the age of 54, after 30+ years in the corporate world, Joyce suddenly found herself living alone and diagnosed with a chronic medical condition which resulted in her losing her job. Since then she has battled with loneliness, low self-esteem, and addictions. With the help of friends, she has turned her life around, grown in her faith, set up 3 businesses, and now uses her  experiences to help other seasoned women make the most of their lives.

WINS: in the last 6 years

• Joyce set up 3 businesses

• Picked herself up and tried again when one failed

• She was co-author of an international bestseller

• Appointed Trustee of a local charity

• Appointed to the board of a local community development trust.

WEBSITE: www.thereignitedwoman.com
EMAIL: joyce@thereignitedwoman.com

facebook.com/thereignitedwoman
instagram.com/the_reignited_woman
linkedin.com/joyce-hardie

THE STORY OF WHO I BECAME ON MY WAY TO ENTREPRENEURSHIP

BY MARY MUNTEH

I don't remember what I was doing that day when I first noticed the word ENTREPRENEUR. It is possible that I might have taken a break from writing a progress note after seeing one of my therapy clients. Or, I might have been reading an article about trauma, trying to understand what it is; why it affects certain people and not others, why it is so prevalent now, and most importantly for me, how people can heal from it.

Whatever I was doing provided an open door that set me on the path of my greatest adventure so far and I've had many of them.

The article that caught my attention was about the rise of black female entrepreneurs. As I remember it, the image of the black woman in the article was stunning. It seemed to me as I looked at the photo that her makeup was impeccable, her hair was slick like fine oil, draping down her back and shoulders in silky lines that left me mesmerized for a few seconds.

I had seen black women entrepreneurs in photos before but this one seared its memory into my heart and brain. I had such a visceral reaction to the title of the story and to her beautiful photo. For a split second I thought I could be one of those black female entrepre-neurs, but almost as fast as the thought appeared the nay saying thoughts came rushing in. However, instead of passing through they stayed and plagued me for longer than I can fully remember.

The stream of negative thoughts was fast and furious, like the big river that ran through my village in Cameroon, moving large stones, trees, and crops that were washed away from farms. Just like that roaring river, without much warning, I felt a tinge of fear that turned into terror. In words it would sound like this: "There's no way on earth that I can ever dress like that sleek black woman."

The noise in my head grew louder as I started to nit-pick at myself from all angles. "My hair is short." "I have no makeup and don't even know how to put it on." That last negative thought opened up the can of worms that brought out all my internal judgements about women who wore makeup.

At the time I had this idea that makeup was unnecessary, and black women were spending too much money and time on their hair and makeup. Obviously, I kept my hair short and didn't wear makeup to justify my internal hellish monologue, even though no one would have known from the way I conducted myself externally, as a fake non-judgmental person. While in my head I had many unruly judg-mental ideas such as, "Women who wore it were insecure, didn't like themselves, and were doing it as part of conforming to the demands of the patriarchy."

In addition, I'd activated all these stale, old, and toxic ideas that I hadn't really taken time to examine before this point. Makeup was bad for women, taking care of hair was vain, and saving money was better than loving yourself, etc.

While I still believe that spending within one's means is important, I'm grateful that this journey revealed the staleness within me. I'm even more excited about the healing I have experienced along the way.

Thank goodness that several weeks later I got curious again and continued to google entrepreneurship from time to time to learn about it. The process softened my mind and heart, and at some point, my brain started to develop a vague understanding.

Interestingly, most of what I believed was entrepreneurship continued to reflect my fears and idealization that I held unknowingly. Vaguely, I thought of entrepreneurship as something difficult to do, but freeing and liberating because I would become my own boss and earn limitless money doing things I enjoyed.

The deeper I went in my curious hunt the more I saw women business owners online, mostly coaches, flaunting their beautiful lifestyles in photos, talking about making 10K a month and helping others to do the same. Me, making 10K a month felt intoxicating sometimes!

I wanted it quick and easy, mostly to make a difference in the world in big ways, but also to show others that I can do it. And that is how I became poised at the beginning of the journey to become a 10k monthly earner without knowing exactly what service I was going to offer. I went ahead and signed up for my very first entrepreneurial coaching course.

Before I tell you about that course, I have some juicy stuff I think you might want to know.

In case you're wondering why I had such a negative reaction to entrepreneurship here is the background.

At the time I saw that article on the yahoo news feed, I was finishing up my doctoral studies in clinical psychology. My training didn't prepare me to run a business or create one. Graduate schools are not generally expected to teach students how to make money. Some try to teach you how to serve powerfully, but if you want to serve and make money you have to learn the skills or enroll in an MBA or some degree with a business side to it.

For six years in graduate school, I'd been preparing to work for someone else. I did my best to be ready to work either in a University Counseling Center, a Community Mental Health Clinic, or for some organization that was willing to hire me. It was important for me to find one of those institutions because I was an international student from Cameroon studying in the USA.

After my studies I was allowed to work legally in the USA for one year. Because I wanted to continue living and working in America, I needed an employer who could hire me. If they liked my work enough, they could apply for the H1B visa which will allow me to work legally in the USA. If I was lucky, the same employer would sponsor my Green Card. After all these processes were completed, I could freely think about becoming an entrepreneur.

My journey was as complicated as any but that wasn't going to stop me. I'm one who thrives when there are opportunities to stretch me beyond my comfort zone. Entrepreneurship seemed like a bone I could sink my teeth into and not become overwhelmed with the complexities of my immigration process.

I believe that my subconscious mind was trying to protect me when I first got in touch with the desire to become an entrepreneur through the article with the black woman. I didn't talk to anyone about that desire because it would have sounded just like one of those pie in the sky ideas. Most of my ideas and desires start out exactly like my journey to entrepreneurship, a pie in the sky, always impossible to reach until I accomplish it.

My one regret as I look back now is that I wasn't COMPAS-SIONATE with myself nor was I kind to my fellow womankind. Instead, I was shutting down my desire, attacking, judging, and criticizing photos of beautiful, powerful women online like the one I saw on the yahoo news. And still, I'm grateful for the awareness I gained through all of it.

As if immigration complications weren't enough, I was also in the process of my "divorce" from the community of the Tertiary Sisters of St. Francis. I was in the process of leaving the convent where I had been a Franciscan nun for 25+ years.

I joined the convent immediately after high school in US academic terms when I was 19+ and enjoyed rising through the ranks to leadership positions. While there, I trained new members and led the community effort to renew their constitution.

Yes, we lived by a constitution that provided the dos and don'ts of our life. During my time at the convent the entire international community was asked to renew these guides so that they could more fully express the diversity of its members, and also represent the doctrinal shifts in the church. Without much guidance I led the team that was created to renew the constitution of The Tertiary Sisters of St. Francis.

I went through one of the biggest growth spurts of my life leading this group. I also saw and felt firsthand that the glass ceiling of our institution was rather too low, both in terms of ideas and concepts, but also in terms of experiencing union with God. That shift would eventually lead me to leave the convent.

What??? Why did you leave?

My shortest answer is that I outgrew the convent and in order to continue growing I had to leave. My deepest desire when I became a nun was to find God in my heart, but the red tape of reciting prayers and reading the Bible over and over without enough time to connect to God inside of me became intolerable.

The longer answer to why I left the convent was full of stories laced with feelings of anger, burn out, exhaustion, and fear. I'm amazed when I think about me at that time. There was so much pain in my heart that I still marvel at the fact that it continued to beat. In fact, it murmured for a while, and when the doctors couldn't find anything wrong with it, I started the forgiveness process that ultimately saved me from a heart attack.

To show you how desperate I was, one day, out of a sudden impulse prompted by a survival instinct, I called into Hay House Radio during a live show and talked to the host of the Get Real show, Alan Cohen. He asked me a few questions, but what I remember was the feeling in my body when he said a prayer for me.

Instantly, I knew that I wanted to pray for people the way he did for me that day, and to effect shifts in their bodies just the way I felt. And my ambitious side - which I have come to love dearly - thought I might be able to raise people from the dead, just as Christ did. Be careful what you pray for because some Angel might hear you and take you seriously!

As a nun, I attended holy mass every day and prayed five times a day for myself and the entire world. I traveled to the Middle East to the places where Jesus of the Bible is said to have lived and worked. I spent time in Assisi, the birthplace of St. Francis and Claire of Assisi, but I'd never experienced the power of prayer in the same way I did that day Alan Cohen prayed for me.

Instead, I busied myself with serving other people and hoped that God was going to reward me in some powerful way after I died. I forgot that my happiness was important, and even though I smiled all the time, I didn't feel the joy in my heart anymore. I had no idea when or how I lost connection to my joy. In fact, when I looked around me it seemed ridiculous that I should expect to be joyful from the heart. Life seemed designed to keep everyone on the go except during yearly retreats, which were again, full of prayers. I didn't want to repeat any longer.

I believed that if I was going after my own personal joy, I was doing something against God. The unspoken rule in my world was that if I helped other people to be happy, healthy, and well, that would be enough to make me happy. But instead, I'd met with several obstacles, betrayals, and disappointments that closed my heart, and I didn't know how to open it up from the inside.

So, I carried a stale smile outside, to put other people at ease and also stop them from knowing that I was raging with anger, fear, and confusion inside. It is a miracle to me that from this space I could see a beautiful black woman entrepreneur and still be inspired, even though the inspiration only stirred up the mess I had going on inside of me. It seemed like there was still something alive, even though I felt brittle inside and completely shut off from real contact with myself. I feared anything and anyone that wasn't repeating the doctrines I grew up with and was now teaching other people, but my heart was closing up as the years passed and I could feel it.

Despite my struggle, that black woman's photo, standing in her power and glory, came through to me. After the initial reactions, I found myself feeling more and more drawn to consider being a businesswoman. One thing led to another, and I got on the mailing list of Ocean Robbins to learn from him and his father, John Robbins, at the Food Revolution Summit.

In high school I studied food and nutrition. Do you know the most important thing the education system gave me? It introduced me to nutrients, and the importance of balancing them in the body through selecting foods that provide them.

That foundation made it a no brainer when I came across Ocean's videos about The Food Revolution Summit. Ocean, a friend of Ryan Eliason, introduced me to Ryan Eliason's Visionary Business School (VBS) through his emails. Ryan pulled me toward the entrepreneurial world with his personal story about awakening to mission after he went to India with his high school friends for a study abroad experience. Before I knew it, I was signed up to attend his VBS Conference in San Diego, California.

I will never forget the day Ryan sent out an email with the photos of the Paradise Point Resort & Spa in San Diego, by the water glit-tering with night lights. A similar fear, like the one I'd experienced seeing the Black Female Entrepreneur in the yahoo news article, rose up in me. I panicked and thought that I'd made a mistake. I had no clothes to wear to the event, my hair was short and didn't look like a businesswoman's hair. I imagined women walking in high heels, wearing impeccable make up, standing around and drinking wine, passing out their business cards and talking about things I couldn't understand.

My response this time was a little bit more mature. I asked a colleague at work where I could get business casual clothing and was directed to go to Godman's in Des Moines, Iowa, a 45-minute drive from Ames, the college town where I lived. I mustered the courage to ask another colleague to go with me to the store, to help me pick up clothes I could wear to Ryan's conference in San Diego. The shopping trip was stressful because I didn't quite know what I wanted. I had no idea what colors worked for me, what I liked or didn't like. I hoped that my friend would be able to help me out.

My friend Whitney was patient, kind, and supportive, but it is hard to help someone who doesn't quite know what they want. Outwardly, I acted excited and perky, but within me I was terrified and feeling vulnerable. I still look at some of the clothes I bought that day and smile at the colors and styles. They remind me of how far I have come in a good way. But at the end of the shopping trip that day I was relieved to come home with many pieces of clothes. They allowed me to plan out how to dress during the five days that I was traveling to and from San Diego.

That experience was the first time I sat in a room with people who were either entrepreneurs or wannabes!

It was surreal for me, and although I'd done a lot to prepare, it was nothing like I thought it would be. There were simple people and some more sophisticated than others. It was sometimes spontaneous and often scripted. Ryan was scarce, which made sense, and I did the best I could to make friends but couldn't truly connect the way I wanted to. There were things in my heart that I wanted to share with people, and I had no words.

Meredith, one of the client's coaches, heard me when I did a few minutes of coaching with her, deciding whether or not to commit to a year-long coaching package with Ryan. I don't remember what she asked me, but I remember what I said.

"I want to end suffering in the world."

She believed me, and I cried and felt foolish at the same time, but I was relieved that she believed me. I knew this was the entrepreneurial group I needed to join to start my journey. It wasn't too far above my head and Meredith believed that I could end suffering in the world. That was enough inspiration to keep moving forward.

I committed to an $8,000 coaching package in San Diego because Meredith believed I could end suffering in the world.

On my trip back home, I went through the folder that Ryan and his team had meticulously put together about the one-year program. It inspired and scared me at the same time. I wondered who was going to be my coach and I saw myself becoming an entrepreneur. I wanted to become one of Ryan's success stories. Maybe speak at his events, like one of the three people who spoke about their experi-ences working with Ryan. They talked about taking their businesses to new heights of growth and success financially, and in their personal lives, too.

I salivated when thinking about my future team and all the money that would be flowing into my bank account while I slept. I also felt like I wasn't ready for that kind of success. At the time I was living in a two-bedroom apartment. I had a vision board with a beautiful home and two car garage, and I believed that somewhere between that year and the next two years I was going to be able to buy a house and have a team supporting my work. I came home feeling exhausted but hopeful about my future.

The work of figuring out what my message was and putting myself out there to people proved to be harder than I could have ever imagined.

Prior to attending Ryan's conference and joining his coaching program I had been a part of John Assaraf's program, Neurogym. I used Neurogym to retrain my brain so that I could make the transi-tion from a life where I vowed to live in poverty to one where I wanted to make money through entrepreneurship.

One of the members of the group, named Kay, was already a life coach, and when she offered Neurogym members the opportunity to do one on one coaching I jumped on the offer. On the 1st of Jan that year she called me. During our conversation she asked me, "Do you have the skills that other people need and want?" This question gave me pause and I told her that I was a good therapist and my clients had good results working with me. I told her that I thought the black community needed what I had to offer because there was so much developmental trauma within our community.

The silence between me and her on the phone felt empty. I longed for her to tell me if she thought what I was saying had potential for business or not.

She didn't say anything.

My heart sank and a feeling of despair threatened to rise within me, but I distracted myself and focused on my goal to train my brain and become an entrepreneur. With the nagging question about what I had to offer to my clients, I stumbled into the work of Edward Mannix.

Let me give you some context about why Edward's work through what he calls, "The Compassion Key" was so important to me.

My inspiration to go to graduate school for clinical psychology was because of the experience of a young woman who I met during my work as a trainer at the convent. Her story of sexual trauma drove me to want to help, but right before I left Cameroon for the USA, I experienced emotional upheaval in almost all areas of my life.

On the eve of my departure, I had been given a letter from my boss in Europe with allegations of things I supposedly did wrong for years. I mustered up the courage to invite the leadership of my province to tell me what they knew about these allegations.

I didn't get any clear answers.

I asked them if it was a warning, and my boss denied it and said that she didn't think much of them. These events left me reeling with the awareness and confirmation that I wasn't being appreciated for everything I brought to the table as a member of my convent. In my hand I was holding a symbol of that under-appreciation, $50 handed to me the morning of my departure. This was all my religious family was willing to give me. It was all I had to start my life in America and something inside me felt the pain that was like a sting from a bee searing its pangs into every tissue of my body and soul.

To cope with the sting, I tried to tell myself that I didn't need praise for my work because I was working for God. The internal war within me searched fiercely for healing. Traditional therapy in grad-uate school helped me to get through, but the hurt was sitting smack at the center of my being. Even good therapy couldn't pull it out of me no matter how hard I tried.

The Compassion Key training was like an angel sent from heaven to help me heal my heart. I went for it the moment I sensed that it had power that touched deeper into my flesh than anything else I'd tried up to that point. I listened to Edward present his work in her online show called, Beyond the Ordinary. The show is still hosted by John Burgos and although I don't listen often even now and then I go on and see the speakers and listen to a few free replays on there. I used to listen to the speakers on this show and during the weekend I used the free meditations that were offered on the shows to help me heal my heart. Edwards' ideas appealed to me because he said that compassion was the most powerful healing resource humans had. I was familiar with the work of Kristen Neff and even used parts of it with my clients, but I'd never considered that compassion healed at the level he claimed on that show.

My curiosity increased when I read through his offer which was $97 and I thought I didn't have too much to lose so I bought it and he offered to do a 20 minute call as part of the package. During the call I felt something inside of me that I describe as an angry lion. The energy that moved outside of me felt as real as if it was an earth-quake shaking the foundations of my being. You guessed right, I signed up for his light worker program even against my resistance to the name. I had no idea what lightworker meant and still don't quite know. Over the years I've come to be comfortable putting one foot in front of the other knowing that the thing that I need is going to show up and my focus has turned toward asking my heart and spirit to guide me to recognize it.

It will take a separate book to chronicle each next step that has unfolded for me since I started this journey. The numerous unexpected gifts and transformations have blessed me with an open heart that has become the creative center of the healing energies that flow through me. I have had the honor to serve people in at least five continents with healing that awakens them to embrace their True Self. Through my Compassion & Release Process, as well as Angel Energy Healing people connect to their Higher Self/God and experience flow in healthy relationships with themselves and others, improved physical health, emotional balance, financial wellbeing, and a stronger sense of mission and purpose in life.

I still pinch myself from time to time when I hear people say, "thank you, I feel like myself again" or "I feel like I'm home now." While these words always fill my heart with joy, the best gifts of the journey to entrepreneurship have been the personal transformations, healings and continued growth that I experience on a daily basis. Continued downloads from spirit, God, and with the guidance of my angels, I've created and continue to create processes to "End Suffer-ing" in the world.

My healing service called, "True Self-Alchemy" with the Angels is the pearl that has emerged from this journey that started five years ago. Along the way I have served hundreds of people in one on one healing sessions and in group healing sessions. I'm in the process of providing a high vibrational membership program to enable more entrepreneurs to clear the blocks that are typical to women starting out on this journey at a price that is affordable so that you can get clear about your message faster.

And yes, I use makeup, and my hair is long! And I enjoy being a natural mystic channels powerful healing energy but also who dresses up, drinks wine, and dances wildly.

If you like to connect with me check me out in these spaces online:

I have a gift for you to support you in your daily journey into your True Self!

Self-Love Meditation: 24:30mins

https://us02web.zoom.us/rec/share/1sMfYZPg-85J5aGKkoJ7aT4KEfq-Mtyu6S2t4_u1yfMo3_XLSAQ3yljInb4-X36_.MynNK5xJb4RKzyvq
Access Passcode: 1w@91@e=

Let go of generational & cellular blockages, and life experiences that affect your ability to love yourself. And integrate unconditional self-love to support you to feel renewed sense of love daily. Down-load it and listen to it as often as you like.

ABOUT MARY

Dr. Mary Munteh is an Energy Channel who specializes in helping her clients to heal generational trauma that manifests in a variety of ways including feeling stuck, fearful, numb, sad, low energy, regretful, guilty, and so on, so that they can experience vibrant energy in all areas of their life. Mary is a licensed clinical psychologist, a certified Soul Awakening Energy Worker, A Certified Compassion Key Practitioner, and a teacher and student of  True Self Alchemy. Mary is the founder and CEO of Success Coach; LLC and she has served hundreds of clients from around the world in her 1 on 1 and group energy healing sessions in the past 11+ years. If you like to connect with me check me out in these spaces online:

WEBSITE: https://www.drmarymunteh.com/
FACEBOOK GROUP: True Self Alchemy

 facebook.com/Innersuccesscoach
linkedin.com/in/mary-munteh-90013119

FROM FORECLOSURE TO FINANCIAL FREEDOM
BY ANZA GOODBAR

Life shrinks or expands in proportion to one's courage.

— ANAIS NIN

I grew up in an entrepreneurial home. My father owned an appli-ance store, and my mother owned a video rental store. All of my friends' parents owned businesses, too. As I was growing up, it was not uncommon for me to work in our store on the weekends and during summer vacations.

By the time I was 11, I was working in the summer with our book-keeper learning how to keep ledgers and process payroll. I sat with my dad monthly when he re-ordered stock and reconciled inventory. I handled dispatching and scheduled repairments to go out on service calls.

It was a lot of responsibility for a pre-teen, but it instilled an incred-ible work ethic in me. I learned at an exceedingly early age, that you have the power to control your own destiny. I saw first-hand that the choices you made had a direct impact on the money you could generate

It was through working in my dad's store, that I discovered my love for teaching. Microwave ovens were a new thing when I was growing up. Women wanted to learn how to cook with them and cut down the amount of time they spent in the kitchen. My dad put me in charge of the weekly training classes on Saturday mornings. Each week, I would teach 10-15 women the art of using the microwave to bake cakes, cook eggs, and more.

Little did I know how valuable these experiences would be. At sixteen, I found myself pregnant. My family was not pleased and sent me out into the world to figure things out on my own. After the birth of my son, I started an in-home daycare. I cared for the chil-dren of 2 families and was able to stay at home and raise my son.

From that early age, creating a work- life that gave me the flexi-bility to be at home and raise my kids was extremely important. I already had business experience and that made it possible for me to grow my in-home daycare into a learning center for toddlers and preschoolers.

After my children entered school, I decided to get a 9-to-5 job in corporate America. I felt totally trapped by having to be in one place for an extended length of time. There was almost no flexi-bility and a high expectation that my job would come before my family.

That led me to ministry work, event planning, and eventually, I came full circle to business ownership. I took all of the training classes and certifications I could along the way and found ways to use those skills to climb the success ladder until I found myself at the top with nowhere to go.

I was ready for my next challenge. In 2004, I went into business with my eldest son. We opened a mortgage brokerage firm that catered to a subprime market. Once again, I was able to engage my love for teaching. I developed classes to help families with less than perfect credit pursue the American dream of home-ownership by following proven strategies for paying down debt, removing errors on their credit report, and raising their credit score to a level that enabled them to qualify for a home loan.

Not only was I able to earn a lucrative income, but I was also able to make an impact on the lives of people. I was using my gifts and talents in a way that made a positive difference in the world. I was in total alignment with my passions and purpose.

We continued to experience steady growth and had big plans to take our family-owned business national. We were in the process of becoming a warehouse lender and had licensing applications out in 13 states when the market collapsed.

I was in total disbelief! How does an entire industry fail overnight? Where were the people entrusted with safeguards to keep this from happening? I spent months asking those questions and not finding any tangible answers. My life was in a free fall.

I had just moved into a custom- built home. A home I thought I'd retire in and make memories with my kids and grandkids. But just like a hot knife cuts through butter, my dreams were all dashed.

First one lender, then two, then three closed their doors. I remember sitting at the title company with buyers and sellers waiting for the agent to enter the room with the loan documents. A day that should have been filled with joy, turned into a nightmare when the phone rang and I heard our lender's representative say, "I'm sorry, loan docs are not coming. We closed our doors five minutes ago, and we won't be reopening."

Devastated doesn't even begin to describe the way I felt. It was surreal. At first, we thought it was an anomaly, and that some of the smaller lenders would go out of business, but we never dreamed that some of the largest lenders in the industry would fold.

We hoped against all hope that it was a bubble that would self-correct. We were beyond desperate to find a solution to keep our doors open. We had employees and their families who were counting on us to figure things out and keep their families afloat.

We had plenty of potential clients, but no products to sell to them. We had the difficult task of calling people to let them know that we would not be able to close their loans as the loan programs they qualified for were no longer available. It was heartbreaking.

The pressure was immense. The feeling of failure overwhelmed me. The embarrassment of not being able to figure it out consumed me. I felt like I should be seen this crash coming and somehow preempted it from happening. I felt like a total failure.

We were a small boutique company with a very specific niche. We were too small to compete with global banks. Our clientele didn't have credit scores that supported mainstream banking guidelines. I felt like I was letting our customers down. Many were in temporary loans that would increase in two to three years. I felt helpless and unprepared to offer a solution.

During that time, I met a woman who ran a virtual business. She consistently offered her services to my company, but for the life of me, I didn't see a correlation between what she offered and why my business needed it. I needed people in my office to help answer phones and prepare loan packages for signings. I needed greeters to make our customers feel at home and make them feel comfortable. That couldn't be accomplished by a virtual worker.

Let me tell you, when you have a dramatic change in your circumstances, your perspective shifts completely. All of the sudden the blinders come off and you can see all types of possibilities that eluded you before.

As we continued to cling to hope and look for new avenues to keep our business afloat, I reached out to her and asked if she thought I could do what she did. She said, "Absolutely!" By the end of the month, I had a simple website and email domain set up.

With fear and trepidation in my heart, and just $27 in my pocket, I started a new business. What I thought would be a stop-gap until the mortgage market rebounded turned into a six-figure business in less than 10 months.

I wish I could tell you that I saved my business, and all ended well. That was not the case, I was forced to close the doors and lay off all of our employees. I wish I could tell you that I acted quickly enough to build an income to save my house, but we had put all of our resources into saving our business. The foreclosure notices came and eventually, I had to leave my home.

I was heartbroken and defeated, but I knew I had to pick myself up, dust myself off, and fight my way back by charting a new path forward. Despite the shame and embarrassment, I felt, I was convinced that I had skills and experience that would benefit others.

When I started my virtual business services company, I didn't know what steps to take. This was a brand-new industry and everyone in the online space was making it up as they went along. That season of my life taught me you don't have to know all of the steps; you just have to know the next step. I learned to trust the process by taking action every day until I built up momentum.

With all of my experience in the event planning and mortgage industries, I thought that I would work with event planning companies or large mortgage companies. But that wasn't the path my business took. What I found in my business were women who needed to create systems to scale their businesses.

They say, you spend 25% of your life discovering who you are and 75% reinventing yourself. This became apparent to me as I saw first-hand the issues female entrepreneurs were experiencing. Many were stuck because of their lack of confidence or family support.

They needed more than great products, services, or systems if they wanted to grow multi-million dollar companies. They needed more belief in themselves. They needed to stop self-sabotaging thoughts and behaviors.

I knew what they needed but I didn't feel equipped to help them achieve their goals. I believed if I wanted to scale my business, I needed to make an investment in myself and gain the skills I felt I was lacking to up level my own business.

Up to this point, I had not poured thousands of dollars into my business, but I knew it was something I needed for my own personal and professional development. As a leader, I felt that it is important to lead by example. If you want to see people invest in themselves and their business, you must take the leap and do it in your own life. That investment was the best thing I could have done.

Not only did it increase my own confidence level, but it also changed my mindset about my relationship with money and how to shift to be a value- based buyer versus a price-based buyer. I began to calculate how an ROI would create opportunities and generate more revenue and not just focus on the cost of a program or coach.

That was a pivotal change in how I was growing my business. It was easy to build a six-figure business. But I knew that I would need to make changes in my mindset if I want to scale my business to mid-six or seven figures.

As I look back at 2020, the best thing that could have happened to me was the collapse of the mortgage industry in 2008. It set me on a path of self-discovery and business ownership in an online space. It poised me for success in a time when people were looking for the skills that I had spent nearly a decade honing in on. When COVID hit our country and jobs were being lost and companies were closing their doors, I was in a unique place to help women create income in an unstable economy.

By taking a risk and not following the conventional path, I set myself and my business up for success by creating multiple streams of income in my business. All of which fulfill my passion to serve others and are in alignment with my purpose of empowering women to become the CEO of their life.

Today, I focus on helping women retool their lives to be able to create six- figure businesses based on their passions, experience, and skills so they can be present for their families. As COVID continues to shape the way we do business, it's important to invest in ourselves and reinvest in our businesses.

If you failed in the past, it could be you just weren't ready to walk through the door of opportunity. Apply the lessons you've learned and fail forward, the more you grow, the more you will fail, it's a part of the journey of making your dreams come true.

So, tune out those naysayers in your life and lean into a community of women who are ready to encourage you and walk the journey with you. There is nothing you can't do, if you put your mind to it and take consistent action daily!

It's not too late to change the ending to your story! By making intentional choices each day, you can turn the corner and create a wildly successful life! Are you ready to promote yourself to become the CEO of your life?

Exercise: Journal daily.

Ask yourself these five questions:

1. What would your situation look like if it were easy?

2. Are you on the path of least resistance?

3. Are you showing up as who you want to become? If not, what do you need to do to show up differently?

4. Are you feeding your passions? If not, what do you need to change?

5. Are you in alignment with your purpose? If not, what do you need to do differently?

ABOUT ANZA

Anza Goodbar is a serial entrepreneur, John Maxwell certified coach, trainer, motivational speaker, and best-selling author. After experi-encing financial setbacks in 2008, with just $27 in her bank account, Anza opened up her first online business. Within her first year, she created a thriving six-figure busi-ness. She has designed a business model with multiple streams of  income to recession-proof her revenue possibilities. Today, she helps women whose lives have been interrupted by COVID-19 restructure, retool, and revitalize their life strategies to overcome the challenges that come from working at home and juggling e-learning with their kids. She teaches them how to build a business based on their skills, experience, and passions that provide flexi-bility and financial freedom.

WEBSITE: www.anzagoodbar.com
EMAIL: anza@anzagoodbar.com

f facebook.com/AnzaGoodbarBiz
instagram.com/anzagoodbar

PINK CASTLES AND MAGICAL UNICORNS

BY SOPHIE POWELL

"Be who you are and say what you feel, because those who mind don't matter, and those who matter don't mind."

— BERNARD M. BARUCH

When you are a child your imagination is filled with all of the fantastic things you can dream up. It can be anything you want it to be. Your own little world can be a wonderful place filled with pink castles that sparkle in the sunshine and magical unicorns that fly...

It's a place where you feel safe. It's a place where no one can judge you. This is the magic of youth. You let your mind wander to all of the wonderful things you feel deep inside could actually exist some-where in the real world. But if not, you're happy to play with them in your imagination. Things feel simpler. Your thoughts weren't so complex.

We are all different and so I know your imagination may not have filled your thoughts with so many sparkles, but from my own experiences as a child, I was often living in a land that made me happy. Even though I had my own obstacles to overcome even then, I still could count on my dreams to lift me up and make me feel safe.

As you head into your early adult years you think you have it all figured out. If you're a dreamer like me, you have big plans. Life is exciting and you are ready. Maybe just maybe, you don't expect to fall down so much, because life isn't always that simple or easy.

When Things Get Dark

"Happiness can be found, even in the darkest of times, if one only remembers to turn on the light."

— -J.K. ROWLING

Life has this ability to throw everything at you when you least expect it. I know. I have been there, and I want you to know you are not alone. Together, we can get through anything. That is the magic of community and connecting with those who will lift you up without judgment. I want this chapter to inspire you and hope that my journey inspires you to be you. This is my gift to you.

I know from my intro I made it sound like I was a happy child living life with her head in the clouds, but that was not always the case. I created a safe place for myself in my own imagination because from an incredibly young age I struggled with happiness.

I have Dyspraxia, which is a form of developmental disorder of the brain in children. It is a brain-based motor disorder that causes difficulty in activities requiring coordination and movement.

Back when I was a baby, they didn't know what Dyspraxia was; no one had ever heard of it. Dyspraxia is now believed to affect 10 % of the population, with approximately 2% being severely affected by the condition. I fell within the 2%.

Throughout my childhood this made me feel quite different from all of the other kids I met. Most children start walking at the age of one, they also start talking around that time too. Unfortunately, I didn't begin walking until I was two and I didn't start talking until I was three.

I underwent speech therapy, physiotherapy, and hydrotherapy. Even as a young child I remember how much these therapies exhausted me. Not only that, but I also knew my treatments as well as watching me struggle was awfully hard on my family. I could feel their sadness and exhaustion too.

Doing the normal things that children do did not come easy for me. I struggled and I worked, and, in the end, I triumphed. After all this work I finally built up the strength to walk and progressed with my speech.

Overcoming Dyspraxia was the first of many hurdles' life would throw my way. And with each hurdle, I am proud to say I became more and more of the woman I am today. Although it may not have felt like it while I was sometimes leaping, crawling, or climbing over those hurdles, it was my strength that got me through. It was me. Yes, I have had amazing support from family and friends. Yes, there have been wonderful people in my life. But in the end, I got myself over each and every hurdle.

In my early 20s, I fell into the trap of loving a narcissist. Like most people who fall into this trap, I didn't know he was one right away. In the beginning we were both happy with each other, doing all things that couples do at that age. A few years into the relationship it was as if a dark cloud had rolled over our lives; he changed. It wasn't for the better either. The truth is that I didn't see it when he first changed. I was so in love that I didn't want to.

His aggressive behavior began with verbal abuse. He called me horrible names. He belittled me. He made me feel worthless. He got into my head and made me believe everything he told me I was. I still remember what it felt like every single time he'd say to me: "You are nothing and worth nothing."

He then began to control my actions. I wasn't allowed to do anything he didn't approve of or ask permission for; if I did there would be consequences. My life was taken away from me in an instant by the man I loved, and I felt as though I couldn't do a thing about it.

When I was nineteen, I fell pregnant and I lost the baby after carrying for five months due to the stress and abuse caused by my partner. He was supposed to be the one caring for us. He was supposed to be the one that helps me create a safe home for our growing child, and yet he chose to destroy it.

Soon after my miscarriage, he proposed and promised that it would never happen again. He lied. The abuse stopped briefly, but he couldn't keep it in for long. The constant verbal name-calling, physical abuse, and controlling behavior came back with a vengeance. I got pregnant again and miscarried for a second time.

His response to the second loss was not the same as the first. This time around he didn't care to tell me how sorry he was or how he'd take care of me better next time. He didn't bother to hold me. He wasn't at all worried about my well-being. He was once again thinking about himself, as all narcissists do. You see he had been cheating on me. Let that one sink in: HE HAD BEEN CHEATING ON ME WHILE I WAS PREGNANT!

Do you know what the kicker is?! I let him break up with me! Yes, you read that right; he left me! My emotions were a mess. I didn't know which way was up, but I did know which way was down. My downhill trajectory was steep, and I fell fast.

I very quickly developed severe depression that lasted for quite some time. I was placed by my doctors on a high dose of antide-pressants. Even medicated, however, there was a part of me that didn't want to live anymore. I was completely exhausted.

I began seeing a therapist twice a week to help me get through these darkest moments. The anxiety I was experiencing was unbe-lievable, even to me. I didn't know who I was anymore. I didn't dream anymore. I couldn't see a future. The sparkles were gone, and the unicorns had long since flown away. Have you ever felt like that?

I remember feeling so numb sometimes that I couldn't move my body at all. They were the times when I experienced such horrific panic attacks that I couldn't breathe.

I had them often and was really scared because at the time I was alone. Everyone in my life was either in school or at work. I was barely able to move much less hold down a job and so I wasn't able to work.

I felt so lonely even though I was surrounded by loved ones and friends who supported me when they could. This time of my life brought me right back to my childhood. I could see everyone living their lives and yet I couldn't function in the way that they did. I wondered how I got to where I was. I wanted to scream "WHY

ME????" at the top of my lungs. I was emotionally, physically, and mentally exhausted.

People say a lot of things to help you feel better, like:

- All things heal with time.

- You'll get through this.

- Everything happens for a reason.

I know they were trying to help me, but most of the time hearing these things just made me feel worse.

Setting Myself Free

"It is not how much we have, but how much we enjoy, that makes happiness."

— CHARLES SPURGEON

Then one day something clicked inside me. At the time I didn't know exactly what it was. But whatever it was it gave me a second chance at life. This awakening gave me the opportunity to get to know who I was again. For a good while, I had lost all sense of what being me really felt like. I had morphed into a version of myself I no longer recognized because it was easier than enduring the abuse. I didn't know how to be myself anymore because the real me was in hiding.

Since emerging from underneath that all-consuming dark cloud six years ago, I have been on this lovely journey to find myself. Let me tell you that life is just beginning at 30. But shhh…. don't tell anyone, I am thirty years young now…it's a well-kept secret. Ha! Not really, but if you want to tell me I still look 24, I'll take the compliment!

At this very moment, I am happier than I have ever been. I am now married to a man who treats me like a queen. I have completely come off my medication and no longer have panic attacks in the way that I used to.

What did it take to get here? It's simple really. One day I asked myself what would make me happy. ME! What would make Sophie happy?
Have you ever felt that you can be more?
Have you ever felt you can do more?
Have you ever felt that you're hiding your true self from the world?

I did. And I still do. It takes time to get to know yourself. It takes time to truly understand your authentic self. I had to go deep into myself before I could even stand a chance. You may think it's an easy journey, but in all honesty, it actually isn't. Until you do the work on yourself, you won't understand just how much effort you have to put in.

When I first met my husband, I was still recovering. I remember sitting across from him on our first date and telling him everything. The words kept flowing from my mouth and I couldn't stop them. There was a part of me that thought: "what are you doing?! This guy is going to run far and fast." I couldn't stop. It felt so good, for the first time ever I felt comfortable talking about it.

I know what you are thinking. You are thinking what I was. To be honest a sense of calmness washed over me as I finished my story.

There was no judgment within that moment. I was completely myself. He listened. He let me speak. I didn't have to change who I was. I was me.

It turns out, my open honesty is one of the things my husband loves about me. It is one of the big reasons why we are now together and stronger than ever. He knew the worst of me and what I had been through, and he had just met me. He didn't run screaming from the room. This first moment with my husband was completely different than anything I had ever experienced in my life. The energy and the connection that I felt was something that I can't put into words. I believe everyone has those moments, but you have to feel it to know.

Opening up and expressing how I feel helps me to heal myself. It has helped me in ways I never thought it could. When you release something that you have been carrying for so long you actually feel free. Right now, I feel freer than I've ever felt in my entire life, all because I've given myself permission to express my true self. I've stopped holding myself back from being who I am to please others.

Have you ever had something that you just want to let go of?

Trust me when I say it can be done. It may be a long road, but when you get there, you'll look at yourself in a totally different way. The same way as I have, I have finally found where I need to be. I have found my voice. I have the courage to be who I really am.

Say how you feel! Say it to yourself. Say it to your loved ones. Say it to the universe.

What I have realized is that the universe always has a plan for you. Sometimes you have to go through the rough patches to gain experience and to make sure it will never happen again. In every situation you encounter there is something to learn. It is up to you to see the lesson and do the work.

When I hit rock bottom, I felt like I would never get up. One day I knew I had to. I made the decision not to stay down anymore. I knew it was time for me to rise in ways that I never thought possible for me. Do you know what I learned in the process? That I am stronger than I ever gave myself credit for.

You have the strength too. You just need to give yourself the tools to find it. A couple of things I do for myself regularly are:

1. Go for acupuncture. I find this sets me back to a neutral place emotionally.

2. I have developed a morning meditation practice that helps me to start each day with a positive mindset.

* * *

Loving Life

In 2018 I was diagnosed with Fibromyalgia. **Fibromyalgia** is often triggered by a stressful event, including physical stress or emotional (psychological) stress. Although I am happy, my body has been through so much in this life. There is no cure for Fibromyalgia and so I will continue to live with chronic pain for my entire life.

When my body goes into an emotional rollercoaster, which quite often it still does, even though I have done so much work on myself, I sit with it, breathe through it, and allow myself to have one of those days. I accept myself for who I am while continuing to work on myself.

When first diagnosed and even now, I know there are changes that can always be made. I knew right away that I didn't want to be reliant on drugs to manage my pain for the rest of my life and so I've taken control of my life by changing my habits. I now prioritize going on long walks with my sweet cocker spaniel, Lily. Although

I'm not a flexible person, I've started practicing yoga regularly to stretch my muscles. Another physical activity that really helps with the pain is swimming. Its low impact allows me to exercise without pain. One thing I know for sure is that I'm not allowing fibromyalgia to get to me. My diagnosis will not define me or my life choices. I get to choose, and I choose joy.

If you suffer from chronic pain, how are you managing? Do you let it get to you? Of course, you are going to have those days you are in severe pain and it does bring you down. I totally understand that. I have those days too. However, I believe that if you let the pain control you then you wouldn't have a life.

If I allowed the pain to define me, then I wouldn't have a life at all. There is so much in this world to see and do. I don't want to miss those things. For me, life is about finding happiness no matter what circumstances you are in. You only live once, so embrace what you need to do to find that happiness. If I can find it after all that I have gone through, you can definitely do this too.

For a while now, my husband and I have been longing for that one thing we feel would complete our lives and our family... a **baby**. I am ready and have been trying again, although it hasn't been the easiest of rides considering what I went through when I was younger.

We have had all of the tests done and they show that we are both healthy and able to conceive. Sitting in the gynecology office and being told that our infertility can't be explained literally broke my heart. It took me a while to process it myself as it felt like the response was handing me another problem to solve rather than a solution.

Did you know that one in five couples go through infertility? It just so happens that my husband and I are part of the one in five couples. I have developed coping strategies to help me get through any baby moments that trigger an emotional response. Whether that is someone announcing on Facebook that they are having a baby, or going to a baby shower, I choose to feel my sadness and anxiety and then let it go. Before I developed these strategies, I was all over the place with my emotions.

If you are the one in five as well, I bet you feel this way too when you see a pregnant woman walking by. You might burst into tears or avoid going to baby showers altogether. I totally understand how you feel as I feel that way too. You want to be happy for that cousin, sister, friend, but at the same time, you feel low and quite frankly annoyed that it's not happening for you. It's not easy going through something like this and sometimes people don't quite understand how you actually feel or what is happening. Everyone just says *relax* and it will happen naturally, and to a degree relaxing is a great and useful tool, however, it's easier said than done.

My husband and I start our first cycle of IVF very soon. Although we wanted it to happen naturally, the IVF route is the best option for us. Finding out that I have to go through IVF made me feel like a failure at first. I felt petrified because without knowing what was actually wrong with me meant that I couldn't come up with a clear solution that would produce the results I want. I felt disconnected from everyone around me I completely shut down and went deep within myself.

I am now looking on the positive side. I am grateful that there are options for me. I am grateful for this journey.

How can you find gratitude in your life no matter what challenges you are facing? Your journey is yours and yours alone. You can lean on your support systems, but in the end, the strength to persevere and live your best life is up to you. I believe this begins with grati-tude. What can you be grateful for right now? If it's hard to see past the hurt, pain, anger, or sadness, start small. Did I have a delicious cup of coffee this morning? Can you see a beautiful sunset? Find gratitude and you will begin to heal.

* * *

The Future Is Bright

"I believe in being strong when everything seems to be going wrong. I believe that happy girls are the prettiest girls. I believe that tomorrow is another day, and I believe in miracles".

— AUDREY HEPBURN

As I look into the future, for not just myself but for you as well, I am filled with joy. You have picked up this book and are reading my story because you too want to take control of your life. You want to be your authentic self. You want to say how you feel to whoever needs to hear it.

Since beginning to take control of my life, I am a lot more positive. I smile and laugh more than I ever thought possible. I have found the voice inside me that reminds me every moment of every day that it is okay to be who I am. It's time for you to find that voice inside of you too. Because you are stronger than you think, and you are braver than you ever thought you could be. It's time for you to stop putting yourself down. It's time to show the world who you are. It's time to stop being afraid of being you. Being you is the most powerful thing around.

From my own experience, I have learned that I can't be anyone else. I have to protect my own energy. Life will always provide you with challenges. It's how you deal with them that will define your life.

Find the positive and develop your strategy from there. You've got this!

Writing this chapter is a positive piece to me as it's something that I have never done. Trying new things is good for you, it gives you confidence that you can do anything.

What is something you've always wanted to try, that you've been holding yourself back from? Today is your day to just start!

We have to embrace what we have and create what we want. As you can see, my journey hasn't been easy, but I wouldn't be here right now if I didn't listen to myself, if I didn't change anything. To get to where we want to go and to know who we actually are, we have to change and grow to become that. It takes a lot of strength.

I want you to think about how you would feel if you gave yourself the power to take control of your life.

I have to tell you it is incredibly empowering. It really doesn't matter how long it takes you to get you to where you want to be. Take each day as it comes, and you will be surprised by how much you have grown.

My journey will continue and will be changing on a daily basis. It doesn't matter where we come from, who we are, and what beliefs we have, we are all in this world together. I have a belief that I am being guided in every possible way, I was meant to go through what I have been through in order for me to be the woman I am today. Whatever belief that you may have, don't be afraid of showing it, don't be ashamed of your past. Share yourself in every possible way. There is always someone that would love to hear your story.

I believe that we have choices in life and it's up to us to decide if our actions have a positive or negative impact on our lives.

Make the choice to live your life in your way.

Be who you are.

Say what you feel.

You have the strength.

You have the courage.

Love the life you live!

The biggest lessons I've learned in this world so far are:

● No matter how many disasters you pick yourself up from, you are still you.

● No matter how many times you have failed, you are still your amazing self.

● No matter how many times people try to change you to fit into their own idea of what you should be, you don't have to. You are you!

JUST BE YOU!

You don't have to change for anyone. If unicorns still fly through your imagination after all you've been through in this life, then I applaud you. You can do and be anything you want to! I fully support you.

ABOUT SOPHIE

Sophie Powell is a Fertility Coach. Sophie is passionate about helping other women through their fertility journey, after experiencing the struggles herself she understands how it feels. After working on her mindset through spiritual, emotional, and  physical release she is now able to help other women around her. Sophie is on a mission to help globally women through their own fertility and she really appreciates the demands of it all. Her mission is to help support women who are yearning to be mothers create the absolute best chance of conceiving, making their dreams come true through spiritual, emotional, and physical release.

E-MAIL: fertilitywithsophie@gmail.com

 facebook.com/sophie.rossp

COMING HOME

BY LORA ANNE STRONG

I stood over my son's crib that morning, feeling the toxic residue within my body, from the night before. My body was sick, a familiar feeling I knew so well. My precious child lay before me, sound asleep.

I felt so disconnected, along with shame and guilt weaving through my spirit and a panic attack coming on. At that moment, I ran upstairs, locked myself in the bathroom and fell to my knees, sobbing.

Every inch of my being felt broken.

I've been hungover before, but this was different. I felt poisoned.

My body was done, she was tired of this debilitating struggle.

I was a new mother and yet, here we were **again,** making the same foolish decisions to ingest a toxic substance, that made me feel like I was dying. Why couldn't I be a normal mom; a good mom, a mom that could wake up feeling strong and ready to take care of her children. I sat on the floor that morning, crying out for help, to something that could fix me.

This was the beginning of my journey. The beginning of, *coming home.*

That was almost 24 years ago.

As a child, the image of a **HOME** was hugely different from the one I know today. I grew up in a toxic environment. There was sexual, physical and emotional abuse at the hands of the father figure in my life. There were zero boundaries and so much confusion.

I can't recall much, but I now know, it's not NORMAL, for a child to be forced to massage a grown adult's genitals, before she goes to school. This is where I learned to split in two, so I could do what I needed to do, without being present. I knew there was something wrong, but I was too scared to say anything. I remember, sitting at a table and going through the multiplications tables and every time I got the answer wrong, my hands were beaten with a belt, by my stepfather.

After visiting my biological father, he would drop me off and I'd run to the back room and peer out the window, silently crying, "Please don't leave me daddy." I hated being there. I wanted someone to protect me.

My mother once fled in the middle of the night, trying to escape, and took my sister, leaving me behind. I didn't understand. Why wasn't I chosen? How could she leave me? Didn't she know, he was a bad person and made me do things, a child shouldn't be doing?

That wound followed me into my adult years. **Being left behind**, feeling as if I wasn't good enough to protect. Not valued. Not as important, as everyone else.

Over the years, I searched for comfort in relationships, food, alcohol, and material possessions. I searched for safety, but instead I ended up creating the same environment I grew up in. I confused sex with being loved. I didn't know then, but it was because of sexual abuse at an early age, that I continued the patterns of code-pendency, into my adult years.

The drama felt like love. It was something I needed. A warm blanket that eventually crushed my soul.

My drinking escalated in my 20's. I was lost. I worked for a club owner that I trusted and ended up being raped by him and a group of men, while in a black out. At the time, I just got up, dusted myself off and continued to numb out.

My first marriage was a haze of drinking, I can barely recall. We met in a bar and as far as drinking went, we were soulmates. I gave birth to my daughter on July 26th, 1985, she was the sweetest, most loving, gift in my life. I definitely wasn't ready for motherhood. Hell, I wasn't ready for ADULTHOOD either! Admittedly, I stum-bled my way through motherhood.

My second marriage was a whirlwind, from the start. He was married. We met in a New Jersey strip club and the stage was set. He was obsessed and I was impressed with the attention, flowers and expensive gifts. He was desperately trying to win me over.

Soon after we met, I became pregnant with my second child, a son. There was a lot of drama and anger, since he was married at the time.

I chose to go through with the pregnancy, even though life was a chaotic mess.

Years later, I decided to leave the marriage, now with 3 children and no real plan.

At first, I was filled with so much excitement. I was single and ready to mingle! I was in search of my, "SOULMATE." I knew he was out there, the one that was going to save me and show the world, how amazing I am!

The years that followed were tumultuous. An UNEARTHING OF EVERYTHING! I felt even more broken, an outcast, and less than. I didn't know where I belonged any longer.

I started believing the things my ex said to me and allowed these words to become my truth. How could they be untrue? I was divorced now, living in a smaller home, not going on expensive vacations, and I was struggling with this new life.

I was constantly putting out fires and never felt so alone. I was emotionally, physically and spiritually exhausted. Everything was falling apart.

This was the beginning of my "**Unfolding.**"

The unraveling of a life, I once knew.

A shift was happening within my life. The end of a chapter.

I laid in bed one afternoon, feeling completely shook and wanted to give up. I was tired of trying to hold it all together. I was tired of hurting. I was tired of life. For a moment, I thought, *"If I disappeared,* all of the worries, debt, and shame, would go away. I would no longer be a burden to anyone.

That lasted for a few minutes, until I realized, I had to start fighting for the life I wanted. I had to begin reclaiming, rebuilding, and reprogramming! I was done living, within this story. I was suffocating. I had to take responsibility for my happiness, for my thoughts, and my energy. No person, thing, or drink was going to give that to me. I had to get the hell up and find a way and if I couldn't, **I HAD TO CREATE ONE!**

It was time to take back my power and RISE.

Let's be clear; the rising part took time. There were plenty of tears, falling flat on my face, feeling sorry for myself. Choosing to face my fears and being able to focus on me, was one of the BEST GIFTS, I'd given myself, in a very long time.

After any life-changing event, in my case, a divorce, we get to a place where we must redefine our lives. Figure out, where we're headed and how to begin the healing process.

The process is a messy one and one that we must be patient with. Healing happens in stages.

Who am I NOW?

Where am I headed?

How can I heal?

How can I feel whole again?

What is true for me today and what do I want to create moving forward?

The purging begins.

I decided to leave behind the home I bought after my divorce. It was time. Towards the end, there was a lot of negative energy within those walls and I needed to create space, in order to heal.

I was done with this chapter.

I hired a realtor and walked through my fears of allowing other people into my home. For years, I carried a lot of shame around being in this home, because it represented the aftermath of the divorce. My basement had also flooded, a couple of years prior and I felt embarrassed for anyone to see it.

I remember having my first few showings, I felt so much anxiety around people going into my basement! I remember thinking, *"What will they think?"*

I returned home after these showings and was relieved! I got through it!! I survived people walking through my home; and with each passing day, till it was sold, I became stronger through this process of acceptance and letting go.

Letting go of what was, acceptance of what was, and creating new pathways, with each brave step forward.

I finally sold my home, to a beautiful couple, that allowed me to stay in the home after closing, until I settled on my townhome! So much gratitude for their compassion and understanding.

When I moved into this new space, it already had a positive impact on my spirit. I felt, **"at peace"**, immediately. I had been living in fight or flight, for the longest. time, waiting for the next bomb to drop. Part of my healing required me to heal my sympathetic nervous system.

Before bed one night, I gently whispered to myself, "Breath, this is your time now, you are safe."

Soon after I moved in, I signed up for a Bikini competition, at 55!

This was something I've always wanted to do, but fear and doubt held me back. Not anymore, this time I was ALL IN!!!

I put together my training program and worked my ass off, for 14 weeks. Working out had always been one of the things that would ground me and quiet the noise during chaotic times. I needed this. I stepped on stage on November 7, 2015 and brought home 3 trophies! But most of all, I brought home a piece of myself I had forgotten.

On this path of, *"coming home"*, I decided I needed to release something that had also held me back most of my life, and that was alcohol. I knew, in order to rise and step into this next chapter, the booze needed to go.

For me, alcohol just subtracted from my life and I was tired of allowing things and energy into my world that took from me. So, on 12/12/15, I made the decision to not drink any longer.

Releasing alcohol, made space for more light and healing, to flow into my life and so it did!

I got to work and signed up for every course and coaching program that came across my email or newsfeed! I was hungry for growth!

I received the certifications and started hosting local workshops for women. This was a scary process, but I put together my presenta-tion and walked through the fear, one workshop at a time! I was filled with so much gratitude for the opportunity to hold space for these women.

This process of stepping into the coaching world, encouraged me to continue the unearthing of my own life.

During this time, I created a few digital programs, and hosted a RETREAT with an amazing woman, in Massachusetts! Such a beautiful experience, I will never forget.

I drove home from that retreat and remembered crying tears of joy. Tears of love for the pieces inside of me, that have been forgotten. Tears of gratitude for the women that said *YES,* to their transforma-tion. I was stepping into this new chapter of my life, that I never thought would be possible! **I WAS MANIFESTING ALL OF IT!** I was taking responsibility for my happiness.

This was the *Unfolding.*

It all starts and ends, with believing in myself. Something I wasn't raised with. The energy that felt like home was, lack, scarcity, trauma, unworthiness, and fear.

When you have experienced any type of trauma, it lives within our body. For me, my healing was to let the child within know, that she was safe. When I began feeling this, I was able to spread my wings; I was able to fly.

I was asked to write a piece for my friend's blog and would love to share with you here:

I assured her, I would protect her.
I would reparent and hold space for her.
I wouldn't allow anyone to harm her again.
I'd even check under the bed every night for her.
She still didn't believe.
Until one day,
She watched me stand tall...
step through my own fears and own my life.
All of it!
The darkness, the abuse, the pain and unworthiness that
followed a divorce.
She watched me stand up to those that continued to manipulate.
She watched me heal.
She saw me, reclaiming my body, from all of the abuse and
the unhealthy ways, I gave myself away.
She watched me take back my power and fucking SHINE!!!
And she began trusting and started to emerge from the
darkest corners.
She started to dance and she stopped,
holding
her
breath.

She thanked me for fighting for her;
For having the courage to face the demons and the perpetra-
tors, who stole her innocence.
My child, you are seen, heard, loved and safe.
Always. xo

It's a beautiful process of magic, destruction, love, healing and creation. All of it. There's no perfection, but there is growth, awareness and gratitude!

So, what does my life feel like today?

This is the part, I tell you, I have it all figured out and life is perfect!

Not exactly.

I've worked hard to deconstruct everything I was taught and build my own solid foundation.

A foundation, where I feel safe, seen & heard. A foundation where I feel pure gratitude in my heart and the breath in my body for my life today!

Everything I once thought, would bring me joy, peace, happiness, and abundance never did.

And if it did, it was short-lived.

It's been a dance. A dance where sometimes, there is no partner, and you must figure out a way to make it flow. A dance where you may have fallen, numerous times, trying to learn the steps.

A dance, where you get up and try again. A dance in which you
NEVER GIVE UP!

Coming out of any relationship can turn your world upside down. A life we once knew, is over. We are scrambling to make our lives look as normal as possible, while struggling to find our way back.

And there's no going back to what was. We learn as time goes on, to create our new life, with those broken pieces. We eventually find ourselves smiling again, loving our lives, and sometimes, even more!

Today, I choose to heal. For me. For the planet. For the collective.

Today, I can say to those that have caused me harm, who have sexually abused me as a child and adult: *I forgive you; It all, has led to my RISING.*

Today, I hold space for others, along on their journey of, ***COMING BACK HOME.***

My mission is to show others they can heal and create something beautiful from the darkest places of their lives.

My hope is that through my opening up and sharing my experi-ences, this gives you the courage to open the door, to your own healing and to know, you are not alone.

You are freaking WORTHY of an amazing life and You can rewrite your story!

You get to choose something different, starting TODAY!

You get to begin again.

I know you can see her, feel her and almost touch her...

The YOU, that is waiting to be "born."

The YOU, that wants to "come "home."

The YOU, that is waiting to shine.

The YOU, that gave away pieces of herself to those who didn't deserve her.

You've hidden her, pushed her away, numbed out, and forgot about her, but she is still there, *waiting*.

Waiting to take your hand.

Waiting to Rise!

She wants you to know, she loves you and hasn't forgotten how amazing you are!

She's been there all along; through the darkness, the tears, the pain and the broken dreams.

She's been there holding you and wanting you to know, **YOU ARE MORE THAN YOU CAN EVER IMAGINE!**

She's waiting for you to open the door and **TO TAKE THAT LEAP AND CREATE THE STORY YOU'VE IMAGINED!!**

The story where you heal. *The story, where you take back those pieces that were stolen and rise higher than ever before!*

We must let go of the life we had planned, so we may accept the one that is waiting for us.

If you have lost your way, please know that you are not alone.

I know that some of it won't make any sense right now, but please keep going.

Be patient with yourself. This process takes time. When we say yes, to our expansion, "shit will hit the fan" and some things may never be the same again. And that can be beautiful.

Through all of this, we start believing again. Our lives begin to shift.

Find your people, even if it's just one human, to witness you, to hear you, to hold space for you.

I know, the road less traveled can be scary, but it's the most rewarding journey one will ever embark upon.

There are so many gifts INSIDE the solitude and the suffering. We begin to awaken, to the beauty of all, that can be. As we heal, we no longer have to fight, we can let down our guard, surrender and bask in the beauty of knowing, you are a beautiful masterpiece, as you are TODAY!

Be still and listen.

Your soul knows the way *HOME.*

I believe in you!

Lora Anne Strong xo

Some love & inspiration on your journey of, *Come Home:*

1. Get clear on what you may need to heal/forgive.

2. Create a plan for your healing journey. (This may sound strange, but without a plan, many of us don't follow through.)

3. Gather your tools. And use them often. (Find what resonates with you; journaling, a coach, talk therapy, music therapy, movement, yoga, meditation, etc., Create your support system.)

4. Do the work. Everyday. (Consistency created so much magic in my life.)

5. Keep Going, no matter what. (There will be hard days, pause if you need to.)

6. Give yourself grace. (You're human. We all mess up.)

7. Love yourself through it all.

8. And NEVER GIVE UP!

ABOUT LORA

Lora Anne Strong is a women's transformational coach. She helps women take back their power and heal, through her workshops, retreats and digital programs. She is also the founder of Project Sober, a community for women in recovery. Lora Anne Strong has always been passionate about helping and inspiring others. She leads by example, by stepping outside her own fears and showing others what is  possible, when you take that leap. She had her own massage therapy practice, (For 5 years), took a yoga certification program, dove into personal training and then launched her business, as a spiritual life and transformational coach. She believes, whether it's a major life change; getting sober, healing trauma, getting fit, or in the second half of your life, we need to address the mind, body and spirit, for our healing, empowerment and expansion. A fun fact: She competed in her first Fitness competition at age 55! If you are inter-ested in working with her, or getting more info on her programs, you can email her at **projectsober@loraanne.com**

WEBSITE: www.loraanne.com

(I have some amazing freebies if you sign-up for my Newsletter!)

PROJECT SOBER COMMUNITY:

https://www.facebook.com/groups/1948993442070200

CLIMBING MOUNTAINS & CREATING MAGIC:

https://www.facebook.com/groups/2238105383156418/

MY INNER STRENGTH IS MY FREEDOM

BY MARIA C. KRAUSE

"My Inner Strength is my Freedom." I had this tattooed on my left arm to remind myself every day how strong and powerful I am. To remind myself how much I love living and how much I love being the person I am today.

Karma is a bitch. How many times in your life have you found yourself saying these words when something really painful happened to you?

In the story I am about to share with you, this phrase kept coming back into my head over and over again. I kept asking myself *"what the hell did I do in this life and my past lifetimes to deserve the pain and heartbreak I am going through?"*

Things haven't always been easy in my life, but who can honestly say that their life is filled with roses, smiles, and happiness all the time? I bet you that just like I, you have life stories filled with adventures, ups, downs, success, failure, tears, and laughs. Some might even happen all in one day, right?

Today, hand on my heart, I can say to you that my life is much closer to being filled with roses, smiles, and happiness than it ever was before the moment you are going to read about...

I get to live the life I always wanted, do what I love, and most importantly, love who I am… But just like in the books we read, every happy ending has a beginning, a middle, and a huge lesson learned from it all.

In this book, I chose to share this particular story because it is the one that led me to do what I do today. Although it took me years to heal, I am grateful that it happened. I wouldn't be here, writing to you today otherwise.

Let's start, shall we?

The beginning for me felt much like I feel now. Everything was "perfect." I felt content, happy, successful. Loved. All thanks to the perfect job, the perfect house, the amazing friends, the better relationship with my family and, my all-time achievement: LOVE! I was in love…

I had finally reached that point in my life when I had everything, I ever wanted...Or so I thought...

Have you ever felt those butterflies in your belly just by looking at someone? Feeling your face blushing? Barely being able to say a word.

When I did, all I could think was that there's someone in my life who loves me as deeply and crazily as I love them. A person I wanted to grow old with, sit on a porch, sipping on a green tea while holding hands, and smiling because there's no other place in the world that we'd rather be.

I loved that way once. I felt that nothing nor anyone else mattered but him, the person I wanted to share my whole life with.

But the Universe works in mysterious ways. She has a plan for us, which means that sometimes we don't always get what we want as The Rolling Stones would say.

It was the summer of 2014. I was 36 years young, single, and child-less. I had finally landed a job that I loved and had a beautiful, one-bedroom apartment in my favorite neighbourhood in Dublin. I had been living in this magical city for 8 years at this stage.

I had tons of great friends, an amazing social life, and as a single woman, this was the city to be in. I did what I wanted when I wanted; lived life on my terms and I loved every minute of it. Parties, social gatherings, events; launches and lunches; brunches and dinners. I was always invited, and I was always there, dressed up in my best clothes, high heels, and red lipstick, ready to conquer the world.

The phone never stopped ringing. There was always a party. There was always a friend to hang out with and a new friend to be made. And I was always fun to hang out with, I rarely said no to some more mischief and craziness. I was single, I was free, and I was living it up.

Life couldn't get any better, but… "Surprise!" said the Universe. "Something is missing in your life…Meet John."

For the first time, I was meeting the owner of the place I worked at; the one where I landed my "perfect" job. Remember?

He didn't catch my attention much at first, merely for the fact that he wasn't very polite. But one small thing did catch my eye about him; he had his headphones on, and since I love music, all I could think of was "I wonder what he's listening to…"

But that was about it and I didn't make much of it. After all, I wasn't looking to make any new friends at this job, especially with the owner of the place. I wanted to keep things separate. I liked this job, and I was making a really good income. Keeping this job was my main and only priority, plus — I mentioned before — he wasn't very nice.

Weeks went by and I was doing great. I had been able to pay all my debts and I was back on my feet, and most importantly, I was sticking to my plan, keeping my personal life and work completely separate.

One night, after our shift had finished, I sat with my manager to have a nightcap drink. While she was finishing the paperwork, the owner walked in. This time he seemed a bit more cheerful and chatty than on our first encounter.

He sat with me at the bar and started chatting away, asking me how I was getting on if I liked my new job. While I was answering, a woman stormed in and started yelling at him in pure rage. I didn't know what was going on. She was angry and she wasn't trying to hide it at all. That night I would find out that this woman was his wife and by the looks of it, things weren't going great between them

She yelled, slapped him, and then stormed out again. She was gone as fast as she came in.

There are always 2 sides to a story, but when you only know one of the people involved, that's the side of the story you get. At this point, I only had one side of the story, the one told by him. I felt sorry for him, so I offered to let him crash on my couch, hoping he would say no, but he didn't.

Later on, as my story progresses, I would understand one of the most valuable lessons I had learned from this story… Always look at things from a different perspective and listen to all sides of the story. The first of the many lessons.

Once we got home, I showed him where he could sleep and invited him to a glass of wine. I know what this might read like, I know it because I've been very reluctant to talk about it, for fear of being judged or misinterpreted. Please believe me when I say, I was just trying to help someone who needed some help. That was it.

That night we stayed up until late, talking for hours as if we had known each other our whole lives. There was something so familiar about talking to him that I found it easy to open up and so did he. I was still intrigued by what kind of music he was listening to the first time I saw him — Yep, did I mention I love music already! Now you know I wasn't kidding. This was my chance to ask him.

"*Mystify by INXS*," he said, and he blushed. I burst out laughing, I couldn't stop. I was laughing so much that soon it became contagious and we were both laughing hysterically.

To this day I am not quite sure why I started laughing, maybe the fact that I never thought he would listen to INXS, or the fact that he blushed about it. All I know is that at that very moment, we became inseparable friends.

Just when I thought my life couldn't get better, it did. I had made a new friend who understood me and accepted me as the crazy party woman I was back then, free of judgment which, as a woman, was hard to come by. I was blessed!

Apart from all the amazing things happening in my life, I might add that I was back in college. I was so proud of myself! I had been accepted to study Applied Languages for International Communications. Languages always came easily for me, so I was combining that plus my love for meeting and communicating with people worldwide.

For the first time in my life, I was feeling like a real grown-up. Bills were paid, rent was paid, I had savings. College was taken care of, and I had a best friend with whom I could share all the amazing things that were happening to me.

In between my busy new life as a "grown-up," I would plan to do things with John every chance I had. Dinner, brunches, walks in the park with the dogs. He would tell me about his life, and I would tell him about mine. In some strange way, we were bonded and the more we opened up, the more we discovered similarities in our lives. Pain, disappointment, successes, heartbreaks, wins, all the things that happen to us in life.

His marriage was falling apart. He kept telling me he was trying hard to make it work but was getting nowhere. I was so happy to have a friend that I would listen to, and believe, everything he was telling me.

Except...Two sides to the story!

The signs were there. The signs are always there, we just choose to see what we want to until it's too late.

A few months had passed, and despite his efforts, his wife left him. He was heartbroken, so he did what most people I knew back then did; he went on drinking binges, and drug-infused parties, claiming it was the only way he could cope with his pain. Sometimes I would join him and sometimes I would stand in my role of grown-up and leave before it got too messy.

Unfortunately, that last one didn't happen as often as I would have liked, and soon, I found myself slacking in college, showing up to work as a mess, or not showing up at all.

My friends would question me, ask me what was going on between us and all I could say was that "He's my best friend and he needs me now." I could feel the big question marks, wondering if I was keeping something secret from them.

The truth is, I wasn't. *"Nothing is going on between the two of us, and never will,"* I would say, and I was 100% convinced of it.

But…there is always a but, right?

One night of craziness, mixed with booze and drugs of all types, colors, and tastes. We started kissing. I never knew who started it, but does it matter? Takes two to tango, right? We had crossed the friendship line and the only thing I could think after was, "I just lost the only friend who really gets me… what the fuck?!!!"

It became awkward and uncomfortable being around each other. Neither one of us wanted to talk about what had happened, but we couldn't act as if it didn't either. I wished I had a time machine to turn back time and erase it all away.

It's funny how your life can change so quickly from one second to the next, don't you think?

Whenever my clients tell me that they can't do something or that they are too afraid, I remind them of how quickly things can change. No matter how safe you want to keep your business or even your life, things will happen if they must. You can't control it. What you can do is take the best of it with you and learn from it.

Back to my story…

I wanted to try to go back to before this mess started, so one night I gathered the courage and invited him to join me at a party. I was so nervous; I didn't know whether he'd show up or not. He did a few hours later. Small chat was exchanged, and I kept dancing and talking to other people. Meanwhile, I could see John and one of my girlfriends submerged into what looked like a very deep, mean-ingful conversation. I figured that he probably needed to talk to someone about his divorce and since things had been awkward between us, he found someone else to talk to.

Moments passed, and when they finished chatting, he walked straight up to me and confessed how deeply in love he was with me. I was shocked. All this time I was thinking that he kept avoiding me because he regretted what happened, that he might not want to see me ever again and wished I would just disappear out of his life.

Then I heard, "*I am in love with you.*"

All I could think was, fairy tales can be real, you can fall in love with someone who is your best friend. Until now I thought that only happened in cheesy romantic movies. "Was I in one of these movies now?" I thought; but no, it wasn't a movie.

It was real. It was my life.

I remembered what my friends kept saying to me when I denied that something was going on between the two of us. "*You would be great together! He gets you!*" "*You need someone like him who can match your personality.*" "*You two love doing the same things, you are made for one another!*" ...Geez, now that I think about it, it does sound exactly like one of those cheesy romantic movies.

And it was…

Three months later we were living together. We were inseparable. We went back to being best friends but with all the pluses. Always wrapped up in one another, with a deep connection that made other people jealous. It was *us* against the world, our own little world.

I had never, in my 36 years in this world, felt the way I did when I was with him. He made me feel wanted, important, loved, desired, unique, he made me feel that I was his whole world, and he was mine.

It was us, absolutely in love, like teenagers discovering love for the first time.

But I mentioned before that there are always signs. Part of me saw it and knew it, but I was too blindly in love to admit it.

Overall, I was happy but there was an inner voice that kept shout-ing. "GET THE FUCK OUT OF THERE! YOU KNOW HE'S NO GOOD! HIS WIFE LEFT HIM FOR A REASON!"

These voices were loud, sometimes so loud that I would stare at the ceiling while he was sleeping and wonder if it was all just a dream and it was time I woke up.

I couldn't see it. I couldn't hear it...or better yet, I chose not to.

I was wrapped up in a world where it was just him and me, and I thought it was perfect. We didn't need anyone else, just us.

The signs were following me everywhere I went, until one day in Berlin.

The smell of fake roses in every bathroom of that luxury hotel...I can't get this smell out of my head.

At this stage, my life didn't feel like roses and happiness anymore. I don't know what it felt like, to be honest. He was always making the decisions for us both. I would put my head down and oblige.

Who had I become? I couldn't recognize myself anymore!

He was dictating everything in my life.

Told me to stop wearing heels because it'll make him look shorter. He would get angry if I didn't answer the phone when he called, even when I was in the middle of a class or at work. I was only allowed to hang out with friends as long as he knew where I was at all times. I had to stop talking about things that were of my interest, they were too boring. I stopped seeing my friends. I was too embar-rassed to tell them what was going on.

I was tired of the late-night binges, the alcohol, the drugs. I wanted out but I was so lonely that I kept going back. That was the only life I knew until then and I was too afraid of being on my own.

My self-esteem was shattered. I had lost all confidence in myself. I was feeling alone and abandoned, like a stray dog in the middle of a snowy winter night.

That night in Berlin, I sat in silence at dinner. He was drunk already. Had left the whole day to do God only knows what. I knew better than to ask. He would get annoyed and tell me it wasn't any of my business.

Blah, blah, blah; that's all I could hear throughout dinner. I couldn't wait for it to be over and go back to the hotel. At least there I would have a bathroom to hide in, pretend I was doing my nails or any other girly thing we do in bathrooms that takes us forever.

In the months ahead, bathrooms would turn into my most precious hideout.

Dinner was finally over. We were ready to head back to the hotel but of course, he was still hungry. He had been so busy drinking at dinner that he didn't bother with the food at all. We had to stop at one of those Turkish takeaways on our way to the hotel. When we got there, while I was setting up the table for him, I felt something warm hit my face. I was covered with bits of food, garlic sauce, hot sauce that was stinging my face... and a blanket of anger that didn't belong to me, covered my whole being.

Bathroom. Safe. Go. Hide. Now!

I shut the door behind me and for the first time in 8 months, I could see it all clearly. This wasn't perfect. It wasn't love. I had loved before and it didn't feel anything like what I was feeling now. I broke down in tears and blamed myself for letting someone treat me like this for so long.

From that moment until the day I left him, bathrooms became the only home I knew.

I didn't have the guts to leave him after that incident in Berlin, I wanted to believe that things could go back to the way they once were. I wanted to be an optimist, a dreamer. I wanted my fairy tale story again.

Deep inside, I didn't want to feel like a failure. I was too embarrassed to admit I was wrong and that the signs I had been seeing all along were right.

That flying kebab changed my life. Everything was clear as water. He wasn't the man I made myself believe he was. I could finally see him for who he was and not who I imagined him to be.

I had been living a lie this whole time. I thought I deserved to be happy, so I hid the truth and created my own reality.

All this time I had chosen not to hear the words that were constantly coming out of his mouth; *"You're too much to handle!"* *"You think you're better than everyone else because you're in college."* *"I don't recognize you anymore, you've changed."* *"I wish you were more like her."* *"You don't know how to behave."* *"Stop being so much of YOU, tone it down a bit."* *"People don't really like you."*

I was in my last year in college and I was determined to finish it, no matter what the cost. I was too ashamed to ask for help so I stayed with him.

And then, that night came along when I stood up for myself, I was just so fed up with all the mental and emotional abuse. I couldn't take it anymore. I was tired of not being myself.

I spoke up — out loud! My soul was screaming, letting it all out and I couldn't stop it. To be honest, I didn't want it to stop... That was it. It was time to let go and move on.

I felt this heat across my left cheek. I didn't even see it coming, I was so consumed, getting out everything I had been bottling up for so long that I didn't even notice that hand-slap coming in my direction.

And then the right cheek.

I was still standing but this time I was silent. No sounds came out of my mouth, not even the ones you make when you get hurt.

I turned around, grabbed my keys, and walked out of that door.

I sought shelter with one of my oldest friends, who was kind and compassionate, and who I will be forever grateful for. She encouraged me to call my family and so I did. I called my sister. I needed her help. I wanted and needed to get out of Dublin as soon as possible.

I could barely speak when she picked up the phone. I cried non-stop like a child would do when they get hurt and haven't learned how to speak yet. I was drowning in my own tears.

The only thing that was keeping me sane, college, was now finished. I don't know how I did it in the middle of all that crazi-ness, but I graduated with honors. There was nothing and no one keeping me in Dublin.

A few days later, I was with my sister, and soon after, on my way to see my mother in Argentina.

I got home on the day of my birthday, September 15th. It was just before the start of Spring, my favorite season.

Gosh, I love Spring. Fresh flowers. Leaves coming back in the trees. Fresh grass. The smell of a fresh start.

That was the moment my new life started. Some people might believe that we only have one life, but I disagree. I believe that in this one lifetime, we get the chance to live 1000s more. Just like the chapters of a book, every page you turn is the chance to start over.

My mother could see the pain in my eyes. No matter how much I was trying to hide it, she could feel it. She never asked me what happened, and between you and me, I was so relieved I wouldn't have to tell her what happened. I didn't know how… But she knew. Mothers always know when their children are hurting.

The first days weren't easy. My mind wouldn't stop wondering, overthinking, going back to what had happened to me. I had to keep pinching myself so that I knew I was home, and I was safe.

I didn't know where to start at first, so I did the only thing that felt most familiar to me.

I went through my childhood treasures.

Like most teenagers, I had a secret spot in my bedroom where I kept the things that I didn't even want my best friend to see. In there, I found old journals I used to write in when I wanted to get some-thing out of my system. I always found it easier to write than to speak up. I could express myself better.

I got myself a fresh notebook and a pen and I started writing again. If it worked then, why not try to make it work again.

Like in my teenage days, I wrote down every feeling, every emotion I was going through. I wrote about what had happened to me to try to figure out why. The lessons I had learned from this painful expe-rience. I started to find things I was grateful for, like being with my family and being alive. I was so grateful for that!

There was so much I still wanted to do in my life. There was so much of life left in me and I was going to make it my mission to make the most of it. Live life on my own terms. Accept and love myself as I had never done before.

I was committed to saying YES to life and all it had to give me.

I started doing all the things that used to fill my heart with joy.

I remember how gardening made me feel peaceful, a form of meditation with nature. It calms my mind. No dark thoughts or painful memories, just me and the garden, at peace. Alive.

Books were always my escape, a huge way for me to learn, to see the world through other people's eyes, and to learn about them.

We are all unique and different, and although it might seem we have gone through a similar experience, we have lived it in a quite different way. That's what books taught me, to look at things from a different perspective and let go of judgment.

Going for walks, listening to my favorite music was, and still is, a great way to help me quiet my mind. Sometimes we need to disconnect from it all to be able to see what's in front of us, the good and the bad.

When I gathered the courage to speak up and share my story, I realized that I wasn't the only one. So many other women had gone through similar experiences, some even worse than mine. Some had come through stronger than ever.

Women experiences abuse every day. As you read my story, there is someone in some part of the world reading it too who is living in an abusive relationship. Or is it you?

It might start with a simple argument and then it just keeps escalating.

My friends most often ask me what the hardest part of that relationship was for me.

The mental or physical abuse?

It's a hard question to answer. Both forms of abuse have broken and scarred me. Thankfully not for life, though that's because I made the decision to not let this part of my life define me.

I don't want to be known as the "poor woman" who was abused.

I don't want to be known as a victim.

I don't want to be boxed and labelled by what has happened to me.

This story, as painful and hard as it was, is the story that led me to know that I deserve better and that I am an amazing woman who should be respected, loved, and accepted for who she is.

This is the story that helped me find my strengths. My voice. Myself. My passion.

It's part of me, but it's not me.

Today, I get to live a life I love, doing something I absolutely love.

I became a Spiritual Mindset and Business Mentor, helping female entrepreneurs STAND OUT and OWN THEIR STORY. Help them heal, inspire, and make a bigger impact.

I also host a podcast by the name of Unchain Your Inner Strength, where women share the story that led them to become an entrepreneur, along with their most valuable tips and tools, to help women be more successful in all areas of their lives.

An online magazine was born under the same name, and now this book.

These are all things that, while I was going through the story you just read, I would never have thought a woman like me would ever be able to do. But here I am… and this is only the beginning.

There is someone out there in this world who needs someone to talk to, someone who can understand them without the judgy looks or comments. Someone who can understand that sometimes life gives not what we want, but something even more valuable, the gift to choose how we want to live it.

Writing my story has helped me heal in ways that therapy hasn't. Being able to open this can of worms and share it with you, has given me peace with my past, myself, and the world.

"I have lived 1000s of lives, learned, grown, and I am ready to live 1000s more."

Love, Light, Be

Your Soul Sister, Maria. XXX

Tips on How to Conquer your Day with a Smile

Hey Soul Sister,

Before I leave you to **UNCHAIN YOUR AUTHENTIC SOUL** l, I thought I'll drop some Mindset tools that have personally helped when I had to pick my broken pieces and put them back the way I wanted them to be this time.

I want you to know that no matter what happened before, it's OK. You are human and you are here, in this world, to experience life with everything it has to offer. What you have done in the past, doesn't have to define who you are and who you want to be. It's your choice, make the most of it!

Prior to leading the amazing life, I live now, I used to be on autopilot. All I did was work, party, drink loads, do a bunch of drugs, and occasionally eat and sleep, if I felt like, or if my poor beat-up body would allow me. Not a very purposeful, meaningful, or healthier life at all, right!?

The whole time I thought I was being the cool rock chick that drank like a sailor and party to crazy hours without falling down when in reality, I was destroying myself. I didn't love me; I didn't accept me, and I didn't care what would happen to me next. Once I got out of this toxic lifestyle, my whole world changed.

When you choose the path to heal, re-discover who you are, and fall in love with yourself; your whole world needs to turn upside down and then back up again until you find a harmonious and peaceful balance.

One step a time, one foot in front of the other; and start filling your cup first. Looking after yourself is not selfish, it's necessary. When you take the time to appreciate and care for you first, doing it for others will flow with love and ease, and you'll start attracting people and situations that are aligned with your authentic self.

Karma is not a b*tch. She's not here to harm you, the contrary, is here to help you realize that YOU MATTER and that you deserve to be happy, loved, cared for, and cherished for who you are.

In my story, I shared the first steps I took to start healing myself, figure out who I was, and love my life once again; and you want to hear something funny? ...When I started my coaching business, I had no idea that the steps I had taken to heal myself were the same ones that most Mindset, Holistic, Energy Healing, or even Transformational coaches, were passing on to their clients. As I mentioned in my story, I used to do them when I was younger, it worked then, and it sure works again and again! So, I'll leave you with a few more to follow through. Remember, the key is to be consistent and to try as many times as you need until they become as easy as brushing your teeth every morning.

...And before you say you are not a morning person, trust me when I say, neither was I. There was a time in my life where I used to get up at noon, in time to make it to work. I always made sure to get an evening job, so I had enough hours to get my beauty sleep. To be honest, getting up late, didn't leave me well-rested, quite the opposite, I had to rush everywhere, and I looked like a madwoman (LOL)!

So now, no matter what time I go to sleep -all depending on how many episodes of Grey's Anatomy I want to watch - I make sure to get up at 9 am every morning. And, I got to tell you, it makes a huge difference. I can take my time to wake up, get all my morning routines done and face the day ready with a big smile on my face, no matter what the day has in store for me.

Here are my top 3 daily morning routines that I never ever miss!

First thing, I drink half a liter of warm water with some ginger and lemon juice. That helps hydrate the body and it's great to help prevent flu and digestion problems. And it tastes great!

I proceed by taking my morning vitamins, followed by some simple stretches to warm up my body. Wash my face with some soap and water and apply sun lotion and some aloe vera gel to keep my skin hydrated and radiant.

I learned from Mel Robbins to leave your outfit laid out for the next day. Saves you tons of time that you can spend doing something more meaningful and valuable such as reading at least one page of a book. A few words from a book can change the whole way you feel or look at something. You can learn so much by just reading one page of a book, especially if it's something by Jen Sincero, or Eliza-beth Gilbert, or my all-time favorite, Louise Hay.

All ready and dressed, I put my headphones on, tune in to one of my favorite songs, and I either go for a long hour walk, depending on the weather; and if it's raining or snowy, I do some exercises indoors. You don't have to have a bunch of gear to exercise. I got a jumping rope, some weights, elastic bands, and a yoga mat, that's it. I work out between an hour to an hour and a half. If you don't like hardcore workouts, chose something you enjoy, such as yoga, Pilates, or dancing. Working out shouldn't feel like a chore, it should make you feel good and make sure to thank your body for being healthy and strong.

For me, working out is my form of meditation. It relaxes me and it gives me time to be on my own, which I absolutely love.

After my workout, I grab my journal and write what I am grateful for in my life; followed by my affirmations and my intentions for the day. I like to schedule everything, that way I can manage my time better. I used to work crazy hours on my business until I learned that less is more, so now I make sure to keep it simple but to give it my all when I do it. I became more focused and productive this way.

Gratitude. Affirmations. Intentions. Keep things simple.

The morning is not over yet and I have been up since 8 am. You see how much you can get done just by waking up early!

Try doing these 3 things every morning: get up early, exercise and journal. Your life will improve immensely. You'll get so much done in the day and you won't feel like you never have enough time ever again.

Make sure to follow through for 21 consecutive days, no less than that. The mind needs 21 days to reprogram itself and start getting used to new routines. After that, it will be as easy as brushing your teeth every morning!

I am not going to wish you luck because you don't need it… You are more powerful than you give your credit for! You've got this beautiful!

P.S.: Would love to know how you get on after the 21 days! Drop me an email and tell me all about it. contact@mariackrause.com

ABOUT MARIA

Maria C. Krause is a multi-passionate entrepreneur who loves empowering women worldwide to follow their passion and create a life and business they love. As a Mindset & Business Owner, Maria loves helping entrepreneurs STAND OUT and become more visible, by OWNING and sharing your unique story, inspire, heal, and make a bigger impact in this world. She is  the proud Founder & Owner of Unchain Your Inner Strength podcast and online magazine, both platforms created to help entre-preneurs share their uniqueness. In her 3 successful years in busi-ness, Maria has collaborated with 100s of female entrepreneurs and business owners worldwide. Maria refers to herself as *"your Soul Sister"*, who enjoys meeting new people, making new friends, and connecting with people who might need one another's services or expertise. She believes that the key to success relies on creating real connections, empowering, and helping one another rise. Together we are stronger! Maria also loves organizing events, which might be the Virgo in her. She has hosted 2 successful online summits, along-side some of the most influential women in business today. This year has brought Maria to start her newest project and business adventure with her first book collaboration, UNCHAIN YOUR AUTHENTIC SOUL. This is the first book from an ongoing series that will be published twice a year. The stories behind the entrepreneurs. How Real Women, just like you, turn their deepest pain and fears into their unique superpowers.

"My inner strength is my Freedom"

— *MARIA C. KRAUSE*

Check out my website where you can find Mindset tools and Business Strategies FREEBIES and how I can support you further on your amazing journey. Tune in UNCHAIN YOUR INNER STRENGTH podcast where I bring special guest invites who shared their unique story and most valuable tips to help you become more successful in all areas of your life. And don't forget to check our online magazine, UNCHAIN YOUR INNER STRENGTH. And if you ever want to chat, make a new friend, or find out how can help you Take your Business to the Next Level, you can always find me hanging out on Instagram and Facebook.

Looking forward to meeting you,

Love, Light, Be

Maria. XXX

WEBSITE: www.mariackrause.com

SPOTIFY: Unchain Your Inner Strength

https://open.spotify.com/show/1tioG0Mklsu8dMHNVH4tQw?
si=VzxO5MFpQOePVAFiV15FSA

facebook.com/maria.krause.351
instagram.com/mariackrause
pinterest.com/mariackrause

ACKNOWLEDGMENTS

If there is one thing that I learned in my journey as an entrepreneur is that success is only achievable when we work together. When one rises, we all rise together!

This book wouldn't have been possible without all the women who have said "YES" to owning their story, opening up their hearts, and sharing a part of their story to empower and inspire other women who are going through the same struggles they once have.

Thank you, Anza Goodbar for being a great right-hand woman and looking after all the things I had no idea how to, to be able to publish my first book collaboration. Nadya Siapin and Andreah Barker, thank you for being my extra set of eyes and make this book one to remember. Thanks to Jen Gagnon for being my biz bestie from day one, for all the adventures together, and for the many more to come. Joyce Hardie, Mary Munteh, Claudia Tinnirello, Ceza Ouzonian, Lora Anne Strong, and Sophie Powell Ross, you ladies inspire every day to go after my dreams and become a better person in the process.

Thank you, Angel Burns, for your incredible talent. You read my mind and created exactly what I was looking for, a cover that represents ALL women. You all have a unique story and it's your time, to be heard, to be seen, to roar, and share your truth.

To my mom and my sister, for their love and support, I thank you with all my heart. Although sometimes you wonder what exactly I do on the laptop all day (LOL), you knew that it was definitely something that made my soul spark and for that, I thank you and love to the moon and back infinite times.

To Claire, my Soul Sister, and BFF. Thank you for the endless chats about life. The laughs. The tears. The thought and love you put when you give me a card, I love them! Thank you for understanding me when no one else would. For your raw honesty when I needed the most and most importantly, for accepting me and loving my crazy ass.

Thank you to all the people I have met in my life, to those ones who stayed and those ones that passed by and taught me a thing or two. You all have played a huge role in my life by teaching me a valu-able lesson to which I am forever grateful.

To my clients, for believing in me. Thanks for trusting me to hold your hand on your journey to create a life you love, following your life's purpose, and creating the soulful successful business you were born to lead.

And to you readers, thank you for choosing this book to inspire you and empower you to Unchain Your Authentic Soul and live a life of freedom and fulfillment, loving every part of your being.

Love, Light, Be

Maria. XXX

ABOUT ANGEL BURNS

"Everything I do is to explore the darkness within. How it shapes us. I believe by embracing the darkness we will find true happiness within us. I just happen to paint the connections between light and dark and how that heals." A British-based artist, Angel Burns, is sharing Art History in her own creative style by replicating famous paintings on her face using face paints. She  has reproduced numerous styles from Pop Art; Lichtenstein and Warhol to Surrealist, Frida Kahlo and Dali. Her paintings are part of a year-long project that is being collated into a unique Art History book, 52 FACES. Now available to purchase on Amazon. *"Whilst completing this project, I never thought that face painting during the 30-45 minute sessions would instil so much self-confidence and trust in my ability to pursue my art career and publish an Art History book with a difference," said Angel. "For me, art heals and sparks new growth."*

WEBSITE: www.angel-burns.com

LINK TO BOOK 52 FACES:

We are extremely grateful for your purchase.
The team of UNCHAIN YOUR AUTHENTIC SOUL author, would like to take this
opportunity to donate, in your behalf, to O.U.R., Operation Underground Railroad.
O.U.R. is a non-profit organization that helps fight Trafficking and Child Abuse all
around the world.
In the past 6 years, this charity has rescued 4100 children and helped arrest 2300
traffickers worldwide; and by working in partnership with other organizations, they
have collectively rescued more than 10000 lives who were enslaved, exploited, and at
risk.

O.U.R. mission statement:

"To shine a light worldwide on the global epidemic of child sex trafficking, and
in so doing **rescue** more children from slavery and assist law enforcement to seek
justice for those who violate children."

Thank you, for making a difference in this world.

OPERATION UNDERGROUND RAILROAD

Printed in Great Britain
by Amazon

50116245R00128